Million Dollar Consulting™ Toolkit

Other Works by Alan Weiss

Books
Best Laid Plans
Breaking Through Writer's Block
Getting Started in Consulting (also in Chinese and Russian)
Good Enough Isn't Enough (also in Spanish)
The Great Big Book of Process Visuals
Great Consulting Challenges
How to Acquire Clients
How to Establish a Unique Brand in the Consulting Profession
How to Market, Brand, and Sell Professional Services
How to Sell New Business and Expand Existing Business
How to Write a Proposal That's Accepted Every Time
The Innovation Formula (with Mike Robert) (also in German and Italian)
Life Balance
Managing for Peak Performance (also in German)
Million Dollar Consulting (also in Chinese)
Money Talks (also in Chinese)
Organizational Consulting
Our Emperors Have No Clothes
Process Consulting
The Ultimate Consultant
The Unofficial Guide to Power Management
Value Based Fees

Booklets
Doing Well by Doing Right
How to Maximize Fees
Leadership Every Day
Raising the Bar
Rejoicing in Diversity

Audiocassettes, CDs, Albums
The Consultant's Treasury
The Odd Couple® (with Patricia Fripp)
The One-Day MBA
The One-Day MBA Part II
Winning the Race to the Market

Newsletter
Balancing Act®

Million Dollar Consulting™ Toolkit

Step-by-Step Guidance, Checklists,
Templates, and Samples from
The Million Dollar Consultant

Alan Weiss, PhD

WILEY
John Wiley & Sons, Inc.

For general information on our other products and services please contact our
Customer Care Department within the U.S. at (800) 762-2974, outside the United
States at (317) 572-3993 or fax (317) 572-4002.

Designations used by companies to distinguish their products are often claimed by
trademarks. In all instances where the author or publisher is aware of a claim, the
product names appear in Initial Capital letters. Readers, however, should contact the
appropriate companies for more complete information regarding trademarks and
registration.

Wiley also publishes its books in a variety of electronic formats. Some content that
appears in print may not be available in electronic books. For more information about
Wiley products, visit our web site at www.Wiley.com.

ISBN-13 978-0-471-74027-8 (pbk.)
ISBN-10 0-471-74027-6 (pbk.)

Printed in the United States of America.

10 9 8 7 6 5 4 3 2 1

For Koufax
the white German Shepherd Dog and Buddy Beagle,
more formally Sanford von Koufax of Ebbets
and Buddy Beagle of Las Brisas,
who embrace me in their unending joie de vivre.

CONTENTS

Section 3

Section 4

Section 5

SECTION 10

Maximizing Success 193

APPENDIX

— Acknowledgments —

My gratitude to all of those people who have participated in my Private Roster Mentor Program since its inception in 1996. As in any pursuit, you learn more as the teacher than as the student, and their grand array of professional and personal challenges, as well as their trust in and candor with me, have enabled me to constantly hone my craft and build my skills.

Sincere appreciation to my agent, Jeff Herman, who has placed a half-dozen of my books, including my two best sellers.

INTRODUCTION

During my 20-year career as a solo practitioner who works with major organizations, consulting firms, and other solo practitioners, I've been asked two questions far more than any others: How do I establish value-based fees, and how do I manage my time so that I build a seven-figure practice with no employees and plenty of leisure time?

The first question I've answered in several books and scores of articles and interviews. But the second has never been comprehensively treated until this *Toolkit*.

I've included herein, with my permission for you to appropriate and modify for your purposes (and a web site to visit to download whatever forms you need), checklists, forms, and templates that will save you an enormous amount of time (I estimate more than a month a year) and dramatically enhance your professionalism and productivity. You can read this like a book, or refer to it like a reference manual, or seek out methods to improve still further those areas in which you're already proficient.

There is no particular sequence that's important; the sections are not in any particular order, but instead serve to organize elements within common boundaries. I've tried to provide maximum support with minimum interference. Most elements have a brief narrative explaining the "why," then a checklist, commentary, and one or more templates (where appropriate) to demonstrate the "what" and the "how." The "when," of course, is up to the reader's needs, interests, and, frankly, discipline.

The commentary sections are my biases about what might make the best sense, and I have no financial connection to any of my recommendations (other than perhaps coincidentally owning stock in some of the companies). You needn't follow my specific recommendations, but I think I owe you my best experiences.

My intent is that you use the checklists as appropriate for daily and short-term planning and quality assurance, and use the templates as needed for actual tactical implementation. For example, the templates for creating an article, a follow-up letter, or an invoice can save you hours of time every week.

I stipulate here that you may have some better ideas than I in some of these areas, or can think of additional areas that need treatment (and I urge you to write to me or the publisher so that we may consider these possibilities for future editions), but I believe that there are a dozen or more techniques here that you can use immediately to improve your business and your life. *Hence, the goal is neither all-inclusiveness nor perfection, but merely success.* Select those forms and checklists that improve your approaches, and your success will increase immediately.

Although this is a different type of book for me, that goal of success is a common theme through all of my work. People told me that I could never succeed as an independent consultant, much less make a million dollars and more working out of my home. I didn't believe them, because they had no evidence that I couldn't succeed, and I despise that kind of projected pessimism. They were wrong, *but they would have been right if I hadn't chosen to go my own way.*

I'm here to tell you that you can succeed more than you ever anticipated—more than I have succeeded—if you simply apply those aspects of this book that for you, personally, represent immediate improvement. I'm happy to be on that journey with you, and wish you the same marvelous experiences I've enjoyed in this great profession.

Alan Weiss, PhD
East Greenwich, RI
June, 2005

Office and Practice Management

The material in this section deals with the elements of running your home or remote office, support for your practice, and daily routine. You may choose to skip this part if you already have a lean, mean consulting machine in action, or you may choose to apply it as a quality control check. But if you're just starting out, read carefully and slowly!

EQUIPMENT

The checklist describes the basic and advanced equipment required for a home or remote office. Whether you own, lease, or share some of this equipment is dependent on your personal situation and finances.

There are subcategories where the equipment can be further specified. As a rule, high technology demands ongoing upgrades and replacements, but not constantly, since you will use less than 25 percent of the capabilities of many devices (e.g., people using word processing extensively may not utilize graphics editing, and those with a personal digital assistant (PDA) device may use it to track expenses but not receive e-mail).

Prices are highly volatile, and I won't make an attempt at a budget. However, if you are setting up an office for the first time, assume a $5,000 minimum investment. If you have an existing office, assume an annual $2,500 upgrade/addition cost, and an additional replace cost of about $5,000 every three to five years, depending on your need (or craving) for the latest technological breakthroughs.

Generally, purchasing warranties on equipment is *not* a good investment, since the reliability of machines and technology is good and most warranties that cost extra are nothing more than profit items for the provider (in many cases more lucrative than the equipment sale).

I'm ignoring the obvious: You will need a comfortable chair, roomy desk, organized files, and the like.

EQUIPMENT CHECKLIST

- ❑ Multiline phone:
    - ❑ Two-line minimum.
    - ❑ Conference calling.
    - ❑ Headset.
    - ❑ Speaker.
    - ❑ Speed dial, minimum of 10 lines.
- ❑ Fax machine (if not incorporated into your computer):
    - ❑ Dedicated, separate phone line.
    - ❑ Memory.
    - ❑ Redial and speed dial.
    - ❑ Minimum 50 pages of capacity for printing.
- ❑ Copier:
    - ❑ Minimum six pages per minute.
    - ❑ Accommodates legal and regular paper.
    - ❑ Enlarging and reducing capability.
    - ❑ Single-feed and multifeed capability.

- ❑ Postage meter and electronic scale:
    - ❑ Minimum 15-pound scale that can automatically trigger meter.
    - ❑ Meter refillable via phone line.
    - ❑ Capability for tapes (for packages) as well as envelopes.
    - ❑ Automatic upgrades when rates change.
- ❑ Computer and peripherals:
    - ❑ Maximum storage and speed you can afford.
    - ❑ High-speed Internet connection (preferably cable).
    - ❑ Backup dial-up phone line.
    - ❑ Wireless connection capability for laptop when traveling.
    - ❑ High-speed laser printer.
    - ❑ Automatically searches for and recommends software updates.
    - ❑ Minimum "footprint" or space requirements.
    - ❑ Minimum software requirements:

        Word processing.

        Spread sheet.

        Database filing system.

        Contact management system.

        Graphics creation.

        Two e-mail programs (in case of crash or problems).

        Two browsers (in case of crash or problems).

        Synchronization with your personal digital assistant (PDA).
    - ❑ CD/DVD drive(s).
- ❑ Alternative and optional items that may help considerably:
    - ❑ Television and radio, with VHS capability.
    - ❑ Stereo system.
    - ❑ Small refrigerator.

COMMENTARY

I think that Apple computers are the best investment. On average, you can use one for five years with appropriate upgrades before having to replace it. They don't get viruses and are intuitive, idiot-proof, and absolutely reliable. Apple's service is good, which is all you can expect in the high-tech industry.

Microsoft Office offers a highly convenient suite of software services, useful separately for the average person, but highly integrated for the techie.

Once upon a time it made sense to lease equipment, but today the purchase prices are so reasonable that you might as well buy what you need and simply deduct the expenses from the company receipts. It's easier, for example, to buy a new fax machine than to fix a broken one.

Pitney Bowes owns the postage meter market for all practical purposes. The equipment works well, but the service is mediocre. The best place to buy copiers and fax machines may be Staples.

Make sure you have a backup, old-fashioned dial-up modem connection. That way, if the cable fails, which it can do, you aren't isolated and can still access e-mail and the Internet, albeit much more slowly.

CLIENT FILES

These days files should be physical *and* electronic. You need to retain client publications and reports that are in hard copy (and where scanning is not feasible). However, virtually all correspondence can be captured electronically.

In either medium, organization is everything.

CLIENT FILE CHECKLIST

- ❑ Client name, address, phone number, e-mail, web site.
- ❑ Total contact information for key buyers, recommenders, and relevant others.

❑ Annual report and related public information.

❑ Buyer profile: family, interests, experience, preferences.

❑ Copies of *all* correspondence generated in either direction, including e-mail.

❑ Copy of signed proposal or agreement.

❑ Copies of all invoices and fee check stubs.

❑ Copies of client document requests: Form 1099, nondisclosure forms, and so on.

❑ Notes on individuals met: potential buyers, resistors, sponsors, and so on.

❑ Directions to all sites and office locations, whether obtained from the client or the Internet.

❑ Copies of all expense statements.

❑ All graphics and models created expressly for client (work product).

❑ All graphics previously created by you and used in client's business (proprietary).

❑ Speech notes, requirements, and graphics used.

❑ Accolades, testimonials, and other rave reviews.

❑ Any planned recontact dates.

COMMENTARY

Physical files are still required, despite the computer. They serve as an excellent backup and as a repository for items not easily entered on the computer (e.g., a payment stub from the client, a physical manual, etc.). You may want to take the checklist and actually staple or tape it to the front of your main client file area so that you can ensure a comprehensive file.

I recommend that you retain physical files for three years after ending a client relationship; if the relationship is ongoing, purge older material every other year. Keep all computer and electronic files on a CD or other media indefinitely.

INSURANCE

Counterintuitively, life insurance is not a primary business need, though it's obviously an important part of your life planning. But you have much more of a chance of becoming disabled with disastrous results for your family as a solo practitioner and provider.

Disability insurance, like almost all insurance, is least expensive when purchased through a group. Individual policies can be expensive, but are nonetheless a mandatory business investment (though they need to be paid from after-tax income, not company money, so that the proceeds are tax free if ever needed). Normally, disability policies will pay a maximum of 80 percent of the prior year's (or average of the most recent several years') income. It's important to be vigilant about this, since consulting income can vary so much, especially on one's personal W-2 form. Although more expensive, disability policies that pay benefits until you can resume your prior work, rather than simply resume *any* work, are far superior. Otherwise, you may find your disability payments suspended because you are qualified to work at much lower-paying jobs than your consulting work.

Long-term care (LTC) insurance has become increasingly popular and protects you and your spouse should you become infirm in older age. Policies may provide for extensive home care, with the benefit of avoiding institutionalization and remaining with loved ones. Normally, LTC insurance can be paid for by the firm with pretax money, making it an excellent investment and deductible expense.

Liability insurance protects you should you be sued for negligence, such as a participant injuring himself during a workshop by tripping over a computer power cord you are using. It will also cover you should you break a client's computer, for example.

Malpractice insurance—often called errors and omissions (E&O) insurance—is another mandatory coverage. This protects you should a client sue you for bad advice (e.g., you advise a strategy approach or financial investment that results in a huge loss). In an increasingly litigious society, this coverage is crucial. Moreover, many major organizations (e.g., Hewlett-Packard) won't permit you to work for them unless you show evidence of an in-force E&O policy. Premiums are generally based on the volume of your business.

Make sure that your business equipment is covered by your homeowner's policy if your office is in your home, or by renter's or lessor's policies if you have space in someone else's facility. (That includes shared space that your accountant or attorney is providing for free.) If your homeowner's policy doesn't cover your business equipment, you can usually arrange for either a rider at small extra cost or a separate policy with a firm specializing in such coverage.

Finally, consider personal umbrella coverage. This is usually a several-million-dollar policy at relatively small cost that kicks in when you have a claim against you that exceeds your normal automobile, homeowner's, or other coverage. It is very effective last-resort insurance. (We'll talk about incorporation in Section 8, but for now be aware that you *must* incorporate in some form. You do not want litigants pursuing your personal assets, so you must create a firewall of protection. I've heard even some lawyers claim that incorporation isn't critical for professional services firms. They don't know what they're talking about. Incorporate as a limited liability company, Chapter C corporation, or Subchapter S corporation.)

INSURANCE CHECKLIST

❑ Disability insurance:
  ❑ Automatically renewable until at least age 65.
  ❑ Maximum 90-day waiting period to begin collecting benefits.
  ❑ Pay with personal, after-tax income (cheapest to pay on annual basis).
  ❑ Ensure benefits from all policies will total at least 80 percent of projected income.
  ❑ Choose policy that pays benefits until *regular* job can be reclaimed, not any job.

❏ Long-term care insurance:

   ❏ Allows for home care and 24-hour support.

   ❏ Allows for rehabilitation and therapy.

❏ Liability insurance: covers you on client site and clients visiting your site.

❏ Malpractice insurance:

   ❏ Covers up to prior two years when issued (for delayed claims).

   ❏ Minimum of $1 million in coverage.

   ❏ Coverage in effect if you are in high-risk consulting (finance, mergers, etc.).

❏ Business equipment coverage:

   ❏ Covers all threats (e.g., robbery, power surge, flood, spills, etc.).

   ❏ Covers owned as well as leased equipment.

   ❏ Reasonable deductible (e.g., maximum $500).

❏ Umbrella liability coverage: broadest spectrum of coverage you can arrange (may not cover malpractice).

COMMENTARY

I've had the best experience dealing with insurance brokers who can offer coverage from a wide variety of companies, seeking out the best deal for me. Therefore, my malpractice coverage might be with one company, but my liability coverage with another.

Group coverage is always less expensive, but not always attainable. If you have group disability coverage, for example, make sure the policy allows for transition to a personal policy, even at increased cost, should you leave that group for any reason (or if it disbands or is denied renewal insurance, which sometimes happens to trade associations).

Regularly ask your broker to investigate better deals, since all of these products change periodically due to a competitive market.

Don't stint on insurance coverage of any kind. My experience is that Provident Life provides good individual disability policies, and Philadelphia Indemnity offers competitive malpractice coverage. But if you give your business to just one or two brokers who handle the full array of coverage, you'll probably find the best coverage at the best price.

PROFESSIONAL ASSISTANCE

We all require specialized help. I just love it when someone says, "There's a software package that will allow you to create your own web site or your own PowerPoint slides," because even if I could master the technology, it would require $50,000 of my energy and the results still wouldn't be as good as with a professional. (Can you imagine if someone offered a book such as *The Substitute for a Consultant Book*, which sold for $29.95 and enabled business executives to become their own consultants?)

The checklist details the major types of professional assistance, and my suggestion is that you develop two philosophies:

1. Try to create a long-term relationship to maximize familiarity, speed, best prices, priority treatment, and so forth.

2. Always develop a backup and provide a bit of work in case the first philosophy is undone by circumstances (a rift, they leave the business, larger customers usurp their time, you outgrow them, etc.).

Bear in mind that you're paying for these services, so that even the expert you're employing needs to be sensitive to your objectives and position. The best financial adviser won't be effective if he or she doesn't take the time to understand your family situation, retirement plans, alternative sources of income, investment comfort, and the like.

PROFESSIONAL ASSISTANCE CHECKLIST

❑ Financial planner:

  ❑ Partner in the firm.

  ❑ Face-to-face access when needed.

  ❑ Experienced with self-employed and entrepreneurial.

  ❑ Does not sell anything other than advice.

  ❑ Certified financial planner (CFP) or equivalent certification.

❑ Tax professional:[1]

  ❑ Certified public accountant (CPA).

  ❑ Partner in the firm.

  ❑ Face-to-face access when needed.

  ❑ Experienced with self-employed and entrepreneurial.

  ❑ Does not sell anything other than advice.

  ❑ Proactively suggests tax-savings ideas.

❑ Bookkeeper:

  ❑ Master's or equivalent in accounting.

  ❑ Provides computerized spreadsheets, balances, ledgers.

  ❑ Willing to deal directly with tax professional as needed.

❑ Attorney:

  ❑ Understands solo practices and professional services providers.

  ❑ Can provide trademark and other protection assistance.

  ❑ Partner in the firm.

  ❑ Can provide litigation assistance (e.g., plagiarism claims).

❑ Web designer:

  ❑ Excellent sites created that can serve as references.

  ❑ Can register and perpetuate domain names and ownership.

---

[1]This person may or may not be your financial planner.

To download sample templates and checklists, go to www.summitconsulting.com. For more information, visit www.wiley.com/go/summitconsulting.

- ❏ Can take care of maximum search engine exposure ("meta-tags," etc.).
- ❏ Accessible by phone within a business day.
- ❏ Does all web site work, navigation, and links, but *not* copy (that's your job).
- ❏ Graphics designer:[2]
  - ❏ Evidence of superb work.
  - ❏ Can guarantee reasonable delivery/response times.
  - ❏ Always will provide options from which you can choose.
- ❏ Printer:
  - ❏ Maintains extensive hours of operation.
  - ❏ Can provide duplication while you wait.
  - ❏ Can provide color copies and color printing.
  - ❏ Can accept work and provide work electronically.
  - ❏ Can bind, provide covers, collate, provide inserts, and so on.
- ❏ Travel agent:
  - ❏ Extensive hours.
  - ❏ Finds the best deals.
  - ❏ Available to change plans and reservations during a trip.
  - ❏ Inserts and tracks frequent-flier credits.
  - ❏ Reasonable fees.

COMMENTARY

I've not mentioned specific fees here because you often get what you pay for, but all of the financial and legal people are going to charge by the hour, ranging from $75 to about $250. You're actually better off

---

[2]This is the individual who creates your brochures, publicity pieces, product covers, and the like.

this way, even though it's a dumb way for them to run their own practices because they charge by a time unit, not *value*.

I haven't mentioned the obvious in the checklist, which is to get references and talk to each professional. Never use anyone in the family or someone's uncle Louie.

Your travel agent will probably assess a $25 or so charge for each transaction, since most travel providers have stopped paying commissions. These charges are reimbursable by your client if you're traveling on client business, and are company deductions for taxes in any case if you're traveling for marketing purposes.

You can, of course, make your own reservations through a wide variety of Internet sites, but beware of saving $100 on a ticket at the expense of three hours of your time.

I've found that law firms with a variety of services in one practice are better choices than doing business with separate firms for trademark, incorporation, litigation, and so on. But I do like to use separate firms for tax purposes and investment strategy.

I've also omitted "virtual assistants," those people who are shared resources in a remote location and may do correspondence, billing, follow-up calls, and the like. I find most of them a needless expense who don't represent you well (how can they, when they represent two dozen or more people?) and you're better off with a local part-time student if you absolutely need help with typing, filing, and so on.

Many people will tell you that you can do things such as file for trademark protection over the Internet. But the fact is a good trademark attorney will cost only a few hundred dollars more than the Internet site and will be much more capable of ushering your application through, dealing with challenges, doing a thorough search, and so forth. After all, this is your intellectual property and brand you're trying to establish and protect.

TIME AND SPACE ALLOCATION

The second most popular question I'm asked (after the question about how to set fees based on value) is: "How do I best allocate my time?"

I've found that a physical calendar is vital. That is, electronic devices are inadequate, because they are not constantly in front of you, you can't view a year in one glance, the amount of text is condensed or abbreviated, and so forth.

There is a rubric that you can't deliver and market at the same time. That's totally false, *provided* that you have planned your time and activities well.

Your space allocation needs to maximize your time efficiency and privacy. I've found that even relatively small rooms can become great offices. Keep frequently used files in proximity, but keep infrequently used files in a more remote area (climate-controlled storage, spare room, climate-controlled garage, etc.) so that space isn't wasted.

TIME AND SPACE ALLOCATION CHECKLIST

- ❑ Physical calendar:
  - ❑ One day or one week on each page.
  - ❑ Full year at a glance foldout.
  - ❑ Room for notepaper and personal digital assistant (PDA).
  - ❑ Fits in your briefcase.
- ❑ Furniture:
  - ❑ Comfortable swivel chair.
  - ❑ Desk and credenza with maximum drawer and storage space.[3]
  - ❑ Wall calendar with full year schedule visible.
  - ❑ Files to accommodate hanging folders.
  - ❑ Platforms as needed for fax, copier, stereo, and so on.
  - ❑ Photos, drawings, plants to create aesthetic appeal.
  - ❑ Fully closing door for privacy.

---

[3]Rolltop desks are excellent because they have scores of compartments in which to store things.

- ❑ Monthly files:
  - ❑ Bills, follow-up, projects, in the month before deadline when due.[4]
  - ❑ "To do" folder on desk: contains current projects, daily tasks.
- ❑ Client files:
  - ❑ Electronic by client on computer.
  - ❑ Physical by client in nearby file to hold hard copy.
- ❑ Promotional literature: brochures, press kits, reprints, cards, and the like, readily accessible for mailing.

COMMENTARY

If you're setting up a room from scratch and have the funds, a designer can do wonders. Mine actually asked what kind of equipment I'd be using and designed a curving, built-in credenza under the windows that accommodates all of my electronics, phone, postage meter, and so forth. I can swivel from my desk to the credenza and perform 90 percent of my work without ever having to leave my chair.

I've found that Filofax makes the best personal calendars, and they have space inside for a PDA. I use a Palm PDA for two purposes: to store all contacts and phone numbers, and to track expenses. This is synchronized with my computer, so that expenses are easily printed for reimbursement by clients, and contacts are shared between my PDA and main computer.

Long file drawers that pull out laterally are less intrusive than the traditional files that pull out directly at you, and a unit of four can accommodate your client files, reprint literature, testimonials, financial records, and so on.

Make it clear to your family that when the door is closed you are "at the office" and are not to be disturbed. Use remote controls for the

---

[4]If the deadline is early April, the item should be in the March folder, for example.

stereo or television so that they can be quickly shut off if you want to answer your phone.

These days, voice mail is quite acceptable (as long as messages are promptly returned) and you can usually subscribe to one for about $50 or less a month, complete with options for the caller. These can be remotely accessed while traveling.

Don't skimp on your office. You'll be spending a lot of time there and it therefore must be a comfortable—and comforting—place.

Sales and Marketing

T he material in this section deals with the elements of promoting your value, finding clients, and closing sales.

WEB SITE

Web sites are important marketing tools, but in the vast majority of cases, true corporate buyers aren't surfing the Internet making purchasing decisions. They are buying based on references, referrals, personal contacts, and visibility. Nevertheless, it's important to be on the Web as a consultant for credibility, to gather names, to sell products, to sell to different types of buyers (e.g., individuals seeking coaching help), and so on.

There is one thing worse than not having a web site, and that's having a poor web site. You needn't have a state-of-the-art web site with all the bells and whistles such as streaming video, but you should have one that aesthetically and contextually represents you well and attracts people. One of the key techniques for accomplishing that is to continually provide additional value—new position papers, self-tests, bibliographies, links to other sites—that compels visitors not only *to return frequently* but also *to refer others to the site.*

The number of hits you receive doesn't matter. What does matter is the word of mouth and buzz that you create so that people then contact you directly as a result of the site (which is why you want to ask new contacts, "How did you hear about me?").

A web site is a primary tool, above all, in developing your brand or brands.

WEB SITE CHECKLIST

- ❑ Front or first page (i.e., home page):
    - ❑ Provides your value statement and/or unique selling proposition.
    - ❑ Provides one or more testimonials.
    - ❑ Immediately accessible (no preliminaries to "click here to continue").
    - ❑ Features clear menus to proceed to varying areas.
    - ❑ Minimal text and work for the reader (no long philosophical statements).
- ❑ Navigation:
    - ❑ One click takes visitor to any other page as clearly indicated.
    - ❑ Bottom of any page takes you back to top or to any other page.
- ❑ Value:
    - ❑ Articles, position papers, interviews, and the like are posted regularly.
    - ❑ Visitors can easily request more information and download it for free.
    - ❑ Visitor can leave with useful information, not just about you.
- ❑ Product sales:
    - ❑ Secure site and advertised as such.
    - ❑ Privacy policy stated.

- ❑ "Shopping cart" approach.
- ❑ Return, shipping, and tax policies stated.
- ❑ Accept minimum of American Express, Visa, and Master-Card.
- ❑ Special features:
  - ❑ Optional streaming audio or video downloads to hear/see you in action.
  - ❑ Subscribe to your newsletter if you have one.
  - ❑ Archive past newsletters.

COMMENTARY

Your web site name may or may not reflect your own name and brand, based on availability and other issues. For example, my web site name is the same as my company name, www.summitconsulting.com. However, by using a service such as NameSecure (www.namesecure.com), you can arrange for other entries to be forwarded to your site if people seek you in another fashion. Thus, since my name is so well known and is really my brand today, if someone were to enter www.alan-weiss.com, the person would automatically be forwarded to www.summitconsulting.com. This service costs well under $100 per year.

The secret to a web site that evolves and is of high value is the relationship between you and your web designer. Unless you are a technical whiz yourself, don't attempt to run your own site. Even if you do a half-decent job, it will consume far too much time. (Most web designers charge by the hour and are very inexpensive because the field is so crowded and competitive.)

Here is my rule: You write all the copy and decide what appears, and allow your designer to determine how best to position and present it, and what technology makes the most sense (e.g., animations, drop-down menus, etc.). Obviously, your logo, company colors, and other consistent patterns should be incorporated.

Web sites are organic—they evolve not only as technology evolves but also as your practice evolves. Start with a simple but high-quality base and you can build upon it with ease. Make sure you also purge the site of older material; otherwise you'll create the equivalent of a Web junk closet.

See the Appendix for an example of the home page of my web site, or simply visit www.summitconsulting.com (or www.alanweiss.com!).

E-MAIL

It might seem off to specify what e-mail should look like, but this communications device is often underutilized or brutally tortured.

On an incoming basis, you should use filters to block as much spam as possible, or at least send it to a junk folder where you can quickly review it later (in case something legitimate was accidentally screened out).

On an outgoing basis, you should always have a signature file, so that someone can contact you easily in return *by means other than e-mail if preferred.* I can't tell you how many times people have asked me in an e-mail to send them a product or package, but haven't included their physical address, necessitating further e-mail and inevitable delay. Some potential buyers may want to pick up the phone and call you or visit your web site, but they aren't going to do that if all they have is a return e-mail address.

Also, a signature file allows a brief mention of a product, service, teleconference, or appearance that will be sent with every e-mail, and that means you may reach thousands of people a week, *so that even a 1 percent return rate becomes quite interesting at zero cost.*

Finally, don't uselessly continue threads. It's not necessary to exchange endless "thank you's" and "you're welcome's," nor should you ever send people jokes, cartoons, philosophy, Web warnings (almost all of which are hoaxes), or any other mass mailings. That's a sure way to be placed on *their* junk mail filters.

E-MAIL CHECKLIST

- ❏ Always include a subject line that is relevant and clear.
- ❏ Always include a signature file:
  - ❏ Include name, physical address, phone, fax, web site.
  - ❏ Can include brief promotion of your products and services.

❑ Utilize filters:

  ❑ Create rules for removal to junk folder (e.g., subject "You've Won!").

  ❑ Review junk folder once a day prior to permanent deletion of contents.

❑ Create multiple addresses:

  ❑ Create two or more, one of which goes to only a few friends.

  ❑ Abandon an address if too overwhelmed with spam.

❑ Utilize spell-checkers.

❑ Ensure readable formatting:

  ❑ Use plain text, not HTML, since the latter can scramble contents.

  ❑ Try to use Word files for attachments, which anyone can easily open.

COMMENTARY

Alan Weiss, PhD
President
Summit Consulting Group, Inc.
Box 1009, East Greenwich, RI 02818
Tel.: 401-884-2778
Fax: 401-884-5068

Alan@summitconsulting.com
http://www.summitconsulting.com

Subscribe to our free monthly electronic
newsletter on life balance, Balancing Act®.
Send an e-mail: join-balancingact@summitconsulting.com

Become a member of Alan's Forums, a worldwide
community of entrepreneurs and professionals:
http://www.alansforums.com

Join the Society for Advancement of Consulting:
http://www.consultingsociety.com/index.html

On the preceding page is an example of a signature file. This appears beneath every e-mail I send out, so that readers can contact me in any way that they find convenient (I restate the e-mail address in case they print this out and it is no longer legible on the e-mail itself). Also, I mention three different offers.

Don't bother trying to "unsubscribe" from spam and unwanted e-mail lists. In most cases, this just tells the sender that you are a live address and encourages more spam!

If you do want to send out mass e-mails to people who want to receive them (e.g., a newsletter, updates, promotions, research requests), then use a Listserv provider. This service, which can cost as little as $25 per mailing, is very useful if you have several hundred names or more. Many offer automatic "subscribe" and "unsubscribe" features, so that you don't have to do anything manually. I use DataBack Systems for my newsletter and promotional list, which can be accessed at www.databack.com.

PRESS KIT

What I call a "press kit" is often called a "media kit" or "presentation folder." I don't care. The point is that you need a physical promotional piece to provide to prospects. For those who tell you that an electronic version is sufficient and you don't need anything other than a web site, tell them you won't be asking for their advice again. Buyers like to put their feet up on a table and read, pass things along to others, rip things out, and remove pertinent copies.

You can't do that sitting in front of a PC, and many buyers are amazingly technophobic, anyway.

A press kit is the physical representation of your web site in many ways. Use a large presentation folder, personalized to your needs (e.g., your name, logo, and contact information printed on it). Buy the best quality you can possibly afford, because you will be judged by this image. It will have two huge pockets inside for material, plus a die-cut area for your business card.

Use some semblance of order. In other words, put your position papers and interviews on the left, and your results, bio, testimonials, and so forth on the right. Like the web site, this is an organic device and evolves and grows as you do. It's important to use for qualified leads, leave-behinds when you speak, expanding business within clients, and so forth.

PRESS KIT CHECKLIST

- ❏ Position papers or white papers:
    - ❏ Three to six position papers, of two to six pages each, based on your expertise.
    - ❏ Include your copyright and all contact information.
    - ❏ Nonpromotional and value-laden for the reader.
- ❏ Typical client results: bullet-point list of business outcomes you generate for clients.
- ❏ Array of services: your product and service offerings briefly described.
- ❏ Credibility:
    - ❏ Client testimonials on client letterhead.
    - ❏ Client list.
    - ❏ Case studies or work performed.
    - ❏ References.
    - ❏ Biographical sketch (*not a resume*).
- ❏ Other:
    - ❏ Brochure if you have one.
    - ❏ Business card.
    - ❏ Interviews you have been the subject of.
    - ❏ Awards, honors, certifications.
    - ❏ Sample of your products if you have them.
    - ❏ Product catalog.

COMMENTARY

A sample position paper appears in the Appendix. You should be writing a minimum of one per quarter, and more likely one per month. Add them to your web site and press kit. Make the topics those that lend credibility to your value proposition.

Focus your bio on the experiences and background that most lend credibility to your work. Humor is fine. Academic history is irrelevant, unless you hold a degree important to your work (e.g., an MBA, Ph.D. in organization development, etc.).

If you don't have clients yet, then you won't include a client list but you still can develop testimonials about your character and integrity. The more references and testimonials you have, *the more unlikely any of them will be contacted by a prospect.* You need permission to use a case study from a client, unless you hide the identity, but you don't need permission to list clients merely as clients unless they have expressly forbidden such mention.

No one really cares about your philosophy or methodology. They care about what's in it for them. Consequently, focus on client outcomes and results, not what you do. Make these as dramatic as possible, and try to have testimonials that support those claims.

Your business card is simply a device for future contact. Don't use it as an advertising billboard, make it overly complex, or put your picture on it. And don't include your cell phone number. No business executive you meet is going to give you a card with his or her picture on it and a means to contact them after hours. Emulate your buyers.

Sample Biographical Sketch

ALAN WEISS: BIOGRAPHICAL SKETCH

Alan Weiss is one of those rare people who can say he is a consultant, speaker, and author and mean it. His consulting firm, Summit Consulting Group, Inc., has attracted clients such as Merck, Hewlett-Packard, General Electric, Mercedes-Benz, State Street Corporation, Times Mirror Group, the Federal Reserve, the *New York Times*, and more than 400 other leading organizations. He serves on the boards of directors of the Trinity Repertory Company, a Tony Award–winning New England regional theater, and the Newport (RI) International Film Festival.

His speaking typically includes 50 keynotes a year at major conferences, and he has been a visiting faculty member at Case Western Reserve University, Boston College, Tufts University, St. John's University, the University of Illinois, the Institute of Management Studies, and the University of Georgia Graduate School of Business. He has held an appointment as adjunct professor in the Graduate School of Business at the University of Rhode Island, where he taught courses on advanced management and consulting skills. He holds the record for selling out the highest-priced workshop (on entrepreneurialism) in the 22-year history of New York City's Learning Annex. His PhD is in psychology and he is a member of the American Psychological Society, the American Counseling Association, Division 13 of the American Psychological Association, and the Society for Personality and Social Psychology. He was recently appointed to the board of governors of Harvard University's Center for Mental Health and the Media. He has been keynote speaker for the American Psychological Association on two occasions.

His prolific publishing includes more than 500 articles and 24 books, including his best seller, *Million Dollar Consulting* (from McGraw-Hill). His newest books are *Organizational Development* (John Wiley & Sons) and *Life Balance: How to Convert Professional Success into Personal Happiness* (Jossey-Bass/Pfeiffer). His books have been on the curricula at Villanova University, Temple University, and the Wharton School of Business, and have been translated into German, Italian, Arabic, Spanish, Russian, and Chinese.

He is interviewed and quoted frequently in the media, and is an active member of the American Federation of Television and Radio Artists. His career has taken him to 54 countries and 49 states. (He is afraid to go to North Dakota.) *Success* magazine has cited him in an editorial devoted to his work as "a worldwide expert in executive education." The *New York Post* calls him "one of the most highly regarded independent consultants in America." The National Bureau of Certified Consultants cited him in 2003 as "the foremost consultant and author in the country who is consulting to management." In 2004, the New England chapter of the Institute of Management Consultants bestowed on him their first-ever Lifetime

Achievement Award. He is the winner of the 2004 Axiem Award for Excellence in Audio Presentation.

He once appeared on the popular TV game show *Jeopardy*, where he lost badly in the first round to a dancing waiter from Iowa.

Sample Character Reference

To Whom It May Concern:

This is to confirm that I have known Alan Weiss for over 10 years, both as his attorney and as a colleague in the Rotary and town planning board.

He has consistently comported himself with great professionalism and integrity. I've had the pleasure of watching him lead fund-raising groups, facilitate meetings, and provide volunteer time to various community groups. He is trusted and respected, and many of us have benefited from his counsel and friendship.

Please feel free to contact me should you have further questions.

Sincerely,

Ronald J. Venito, Esq.
Counselor at Law

RJV/ll

PROPOSALS

A proposal is an offer to do business with a client on a formalized basis. It specifies what is to be accomplished, how to measure progress, what the value is to the organization, terms and conditions, and so forth. It is *not* a negotiating document, but rather a summation of conceptual agreement on these issues reached in prior discussions with the buyer.

Proposals can be for small amounts or large, for a brief project or for extended projects, but they should *always* be employed to protect both the consultant and the buyer. Conditions and people may change, but a proposal guarantees certain agreements remain in place unless both sides jointly agree to make changes.

A proposal becomes a legal agreement when both parties sign it. However, I do not favor boilerplate or legalese, because the last thing you want is that your proposal goes to the client's legal department. Hence, you'll see that the example I've provided is in conversational language and is based in previous discussions.

PROPOSAL CHECKLIST

- ❑ Conceptual agreement reached previously:
    - ❑ Objectives: What business outcomes are to be achieved?
    - ❑ Measures: What indicators will demonstrate progress and fulfillment?
    - ❑ Value: What is the impact on the client organization of these objectives?
- ❑ All components completed:
    - ❑ Situation appraisal: What is the reason for the proposal in general?
    - ❑ Objectives.
    - ❑ Measures.
    - ❑ Value.
    - ❑ Timing: What are the anticipated launch and completion dates?
    - ❑ Methodology and options: What are the choices for implementation?
    - ❑ Joint accountabilities: Who is responsible for what?
    - ❑ Terms and conditions: What are the fees and how are they to be paid?
    - ❑ Acceptance: What options are desired and will you agree to these terms?

To download sample templates and checklists, go to www.summitconsulting.com. For more information, visit www.wiley.com/go/summitconsulting.

❑ Logistics completed:

  ❑ FedEx two copies signed by you.

  ❑ Establish in the cover letter your follow-up date to call client.

COMMENTARY

A proposal should be about two to three pages in length, despite the size of the project. Don't include resumes of the staff or other extraneous material. *Proposals are summations, not explorations.*

You'll find that gaining clear conceptual agreement on the contents of the proposal with a buyer prior to committing anything to writing is critical. Also, provide the buyer with options in the proposal, so that the buyer is psychologically considering *"How* should I do this?" instead of just "Should I do this?"

There is never a reason to discuss fees prior to the buyer seeing them in the proposal itself. Be sure to arrange for a clear follow-up date—never rely on the buyer simply calling you back. The longer you wait, the more bad things can occur.

When I gain conceptual agreement first and then use this proposal format, I close 80 percent of my proposals, no matter their size. Feel free to use the proposal template, substituting your own client's situation but conforming to the nine categories.

Proposal Template

PROPOSAL FOR XXX

SITUATION APPRAISAL

You have begun a major reorganization with the intent of improving supervision. You are seeking to ensure at minimum a continuation of the present levels of effectiveness during the approximately six-month transition period, and to improve that effectiveness still further upon completion of the new structure.

To download sample templates and checklists, go to www.summitconsulting.com. For more information, visit www.wiley.com/go/summitconsulting.

The new organization will rely heavily on a matrix management approach, and will necessitate the active support and ownership of virtually all employees at every level for ultimate success. You are seeking objective, skilled, third-party assistance to safeguard the transition and guarantee the efficacy of the approaches used during the transition period. In addition, you require ideas, insights, and proven methods used in similar situations elsewhere to deal with known dynamics such as a somewhat cynical employee base (by nature of the job), perceptions by some of diminished responsibilities, a loss of focus on the work product itself, and so on.

OBJECTIVES

The objectives of this consulting assistance include, but are not limited to:

- Adding value to the supervisory process for XXX.
- Increasing the effectiveness of supervision.
- Securing employee ownership of the changes, especially among formal and informal leadership.
- Bringing to bear world-class techniques from superb organizations that have undergone similar transitions.
- Preventing problems before the more expensive and sometimes embarrassing contingent actions must be used.
- Using the opportunity to improve teamwork, prevent elitism, and build skills in matrix resource sharing and apportionment.
- Institutionalizing knowledge and keeping turnover of needed talent to a minimum.

MEASURES OF SUCCESS

Progress toward the objectives will be measured by:

- Feedback opportunities created for employees to inform management.
- Actual observations and anecdotal information collected by management.
- Anticipation of and responsiveness to supervisory priorities.
- Over the longer term, more effective supervision for XXX.
- Completion of the transition within a six-month period.

Value to XXX

The value of this project appears to be multifold, including:

- Improved supervision.
- Faster and more appropriate responsiveness.
- Protection and retention of key talent.
- Demonstration that major changes can be managed by existing staff without loss of focus or effectiveness on normal priorities.
- Avoidance of productivity loss by employees by focusing on the future and the job outputs, and not the transition and perceived disadvantages.
- Even greater stature in the eyes of XXX.

Timing

The transition itself is estimated to take six months, which is a reasonable expectation, barring unforeseen developments. I am able to begin within a week of your approval, provided that it is forthcoming by mid-February.

Methodology and Options

There are three levels of interaction that can be effective for this project, depending on the degree of help and participation you desire from your consultant.

1. **Advisory.** In this capacity I would serve as your backstage resource, meeting with the small team charged with effecting the transition. The role would include sounding board for plans, idea and technique source for implementation steps, devil's advocate on key moves, third-party objective review source, and facilitator of the transition process itself. We would meet as often as needed and without constraint, I would be constantly accessible by phone and e-mail for document review and advice, and I estimate the time together to encompass about 90 days, or the first half of the transition period.
2. **Consultative.** In addition to the responsibilities and contributions of option #1, I would also work with selected managers, team leaders,

and others to help them individually with their role in the transition and with their accountabilities as exemplars to others; recommend adjustments to systems and procedures that require modification to work optimally within the new structure; attend predetermined work meetings to evaluate the effectiveness of critical elements (e.g., resource sharing, responsiveness, honesty, equality of various elements, etc.); and be available to selected others at their request in addition to the primary team. I estimate that this involvement would last for the duration of the transition period, about six months.

3. **Collaborative.** In addition to the roles described in both options #1 and #2, I would recommend specific work distribution changes; recommend appropriate personnel changes; provide specific skills development and/or counseling to any employees identified as requiring it by the primary team; and XXX. This option includes an audit at a future point determined by you (I suggest six months after the completed transition) to measure results against the baseline previously established. The involvement here would entail about nine months (90 days posttransition completion) and the additional later audit.

Note that all options include unlimited access to my time and help within the parameters described.

JOINT ACCOUNTABILITIES

You would be responsible for internal scheduling, reasonable access to key personnel, on-site administrative support, and reasonable access to past and current documentation that would aid the project. I would sign all required nondisclosure and confidentiality agreements, and would provide all administrative support off-site. We agree to immediately apprise each other of any intelligence or findings that would impact the success of the project so that rapid action could be considered. I am covered by comprehensive errors and omissions insurance.

TERMS AND CONDITIONS

I never assess an hourly or daily fee, since you should not have to make an investment decision every time my assistance may be needed, nor should your people have to seek permission to spend money if they need my help. This is a unique feature of my consulting practice.

Fees for the options are:

Option 1: $45,000.
Option 2: $72,000.
Option 3: $126,000.

These fees are *inclusive* of expenses, so long as all work required is in the general XXX area. All travel, administrative, logistical, and communication expenses are included, so there is no further amount due for any option.

Payment terms for any of the options are:

- Fifty percent due on acceptance of this proposal.
- Fifty percent due 45 days after acceptance.

We offer a courtesy discount of 10 percent when the full fee is paid upon acceptance.

This project, once approved, is noncancelable for any reason, although it may be delayed, rescheduled, and otherwise postponed without any penalty whatsoever. My work is guaranteed. In the event you feel that I am not meeting the standards described herein or based on our mutual conversations and agreements, I will refund your entire fee upon such notification.

ACCEPTANCE

Your signature below indicates acceptance of this proposal and the terms and conditions herein. Alternatively, your initial payment per the terms above will also represent acceptance of this proposal.

Please check the option you prefer: __ #1 __ #2 __ #3

For Summit Consulting Group, Inc.:   For XXX:

Signature: _____   Signature: _____

Name: Alan Weiss, Ph.D.   Name: _____

Title: President   Title: _____

Date: February 3, 200X   Date: _____

Proposal Cancellation Clauses Templates

Note: These may be used for any event or project, from a speech to consulting, and from coaching to facilitation.

- This project is noncancelable for any reason. However, it may be postponed, delayed, and/or rescheduled without penalty or time limit, subject only to mutually agreeable dates and times. All payments must be made per the existing payment schedule in this agreement.
- Cancellation of this project will incur no penalty if made 90 days or more from the start date [event date, etc.]; a penalty of 25 percent if made between 61 and 89 days from that date; a penalty of 50 percent if made between 31 and 59 days of that date; and a 100 percent penalty if made within 30 days of that date. Penalties are due at the time of cancellation. No services are due in the event of such cancellations.
- This project may be canceled by either party without penalty up to 60 days in advance of the commencement date. Subsequent to that date, if you cancel, you agree to pay a 50 percent cancellation fee up to 10 days prior to the event, and a 75 percent cancellation fee within 10 days of the event. If I am unable to provide the services described or must cancel within 60 days of commencement, I will provide a replacement of equal caliber agreeable to you for the existing fees agreed upon, or will return all advance payments made and we will nullify the agreement.

Additional clause for protection and comfort:

- I stand behind and assure you of the quality of my work, and will refund your entire fee if you find evidence that I have not performed in a professional and ethical manner consistent with the actions agreed upon in this document.

An alternative protection clause:

- If you find that the objectives for this project are not being met according to the measures of success that we have agreed upon, I will

To download sample templates and checklists, go to www.summitconsulting.com. For more information, visit www.wiley.com/go/summitconsulting.

continue to work on the project at no additional fee beyond expense reimbursement until we concur that the objectives are met. Failing that, I will refund all fees paid.

Simple Letter of Agreement Template

I'm providing a summary of our discussion of January 19, which outlined the basis for our working relationship for 2005. There are to be 10 areas of involvement:

1. Monthly meetings between the two of us to discuss strategy, longer-term issues, and personal growth goals.
2. Personal development for each business head, based on a series of ongoing meetings I plan with Tim, Frances, Bob, and Brittany. These will be individualized and mutually agreed upon. In addition, I'll serve as a sounding board for them as they work to achieve their business goals. You will apprise them of this support.
3. Partnership with Jim, wherein I will assist him in contributing to the business as a senior manager and internal consultant, not merely as a human resource facilitator. This will focus globally, and will include improving the caliber of human resource professionals and hires. I have already established a preliminary discussion.
4. Responding to other key managers on an as-needed basis. You (or the business heads) will apprise them of this support.
5. Work with Jim to set up and facilitate the next top-level review group, to assess value-added of people and positions.
6. Specifically work with the relevant managers to establish:
   - A succession plan and ensuing development plan.
   - A comprehensive educational plan for the organization.

To download sample templates and checklists, go to www.summitconsulting.com. For more information, visit www.wiley.com/go/summitconsulting.

- Clarity of field management's role, development, and key personnel.
- Sales analysis tools for effectively monitoring and managing business.

7. Situational responsiveness to needs that arise that you deem require my assistance, which are not covered elsewhere.
8. Assistance in the preparation and delivery of the February sales meeting.
9. Working with the relevant managers to strengthen employee communications, particularly in areas of trust, credibility, and recognizing the importance of everyone's contribution.
10. Quarterly meeting with Trevor to provide assistance as he sees fit, including suggestions for what he can be doing to enhance performance.

To accomplish these goals, I will increase my time allocation by about 20 percent. Historically, we've both honored schedules very well, and some months might be close to 75 percent and others 10 percent, but the average will hold.

The total fee will be $100,000, of which $32,500 has already been paid. The remaining $67,500 will be paid in 10 equal installments of $6,750 from March through December. Expenses will be billed monthly, as they are now. I'll provide a monthly summary sheet of focus and results.

Let me know if I've missed anything. I've already received a call from Ron, and I'll be seeing him on some information system (IS) issues in February. I'll also be scheduling our time together with Fran in the next day or so.

It's a pleasure to have somewhere to go once again during such cold weather. . . .

COLD CALLING

Cold calls are not the best way to conduct business prospecting. After all, do you buy securities from the person who calls at 8:30 in the evening and tells you that you're one of the lucky few selected to purchase oil futures in Turzakistonia?

Probably not.

But on occasion it makes sense to call someone whom you believe to be a high-potential prospective buyer. As long as you have to do it, there is an art and a science that can be mastered.[1]

The sequence, deconstructed, looks like this:

1. *Verification* of reaching the person you seek.
2. *Validation* that the person has the relevant responsibility.
3. *Identification* of yourself and your firm.
4. *Investigation* of need.
5. *Rhetorical question* to increase interest.
6. *Testimonial statement* to gain credibility.
7. *Inquiry* to gain involvement.
8. *Assumptive close* with options to move to next step.

Keep your tone conversational and relatively brief. Don't enter into debates or defensive posture. Remember that the next step in this pursuit is a face-to-face meeting, so *never* attempt to sell anything over the phone (this is not a telemarketing script).

Some hints:

- ✔ If you don't get your party, hang up and leave no message at all.
- ✔ Try calling early in the morning, after business hours, and on Saturday morning.
- ✔ Note that you don't need an interaction between each step.
- ✔ Don't take rejection personally—just move on.

---

[1] I've placed a cold call bibliography in the Appendix for those who want to read further on this subject.

COLD CALL CHECKLIST

- ❑ Homework on prospect completed:
    - ❑ Company size, revenues, employment, scope of operations.[2]
    - ❑ Buyer's name, title, responsibilities.
    - ❑ Major products/services/competition.
    - ❑ Clearly articulate the value you could offer.
- ❑ Your environment optimized:
    - ❑ Privacy and comfort.
    - ❑ Positive attitude.
    - ❑ Notes and script ready and readable.
- ❑ Rehearsal completed:
    - ❑ Test your responses with someone else.
    - ❑ Practice the key phrases, questions, and suggestions.

COMMENTARY

It's actually helpful to have a mirror facing you so that you can smile into it while calling. I know it sounds nutty, but smiling eases your facial tension and vocal muscles and tends to eliminate stress in your voice.

Listen to some pleasant music or some comedy just before you call to set the right frame of mind. Remember that you're trying to provide value to a company that needs it, not trying to make a sale. Keep your customer or prospect in mind, not yourself.

Above all, remember that you're trying to obtain a personal meeting, that's all. Don't overreach on the phone. Cold calling is not a good way to market for a living, but it's inevitable that you will have to do it on occasion, so you might as well become proficient at it.

---

[2]You can learn these from public documents, annual reports, and news stories, if a public company; you can learn them from calling the switchboard, an Internet search, and networking if a privately held company.

Cold Call Telephone Script

Note: Your lines are in italic. The numbers relate to the points in the cold call sequence listed earlier.

[1.] *Hello, am I speaking to Donald Lamont?*

Yes.

[2.] *Am I correct that you are responsible for the billing of all medical charges for reimbursement?*

Yes. Who's calling, please?

[3.] *I'm Alan Weiss of Summit Consulting Group.*

[4.] *I'm calling because I understand that you have tremendous pressure on your profit margins, and that improving incorrect practitioner coding is one area of significant potential savings. Is that right?*

Well, that is true. It's one of several areas.

[5.] *Did you know that statistics indicate over 60 percent of practitioners either over code or under code, which can result in both lowered profits and government audits?*

[6.] *We've worked with clients such as Freedom Hospital, New England Physicians Network, and Johnson Managed Care, and have increased reimbursements by more than 30 percent annually through proper coding procedures introduced at the practitioner level.*

[7.] *Would you be interested in learning about some of these techniques, which can be implemented to improve the current year's profits?*

I might. How would that work?

[8.] *I can meet with you next week for breakfast any morning, or during the day Monday through Wednesday, or at the end of the day on Thursday. What's best for you?*

To download sample templates and checklists, go to www.summitconsulting.com. For more information, visit www.wiley.com/go/summitconsulting.

COLD CALL LETTER

Instead of calling, sometimes it makes sense to send a letter first; hence, you will need a "cold call letter." The purpose of the letter is to lead to a telephone call that is no longer "cold" but rather "lukewarm."

Find a potential buyer as you would in the preceding cold call example, but then take the time to compose a letter.

Some hints:

✔ Cite a problem or opportunity currently of importance.

✔ Provide value and whet the appetite.

✔ Remember that you're not trying to make a sale, only to obtain a meeting through a follow-up call.

✔ Follow up promptly with a phone call, as promised.

✔ Consider using FedEx to ensure the letter gets onto the potential buyer's desk.

COLD CALL LETTER CHECKLIST

❑ One page that quickly gets to the point.

❑ Enclose whatever will add credibility but not overwhelm.

❑ Make personal and specific enough to get by secretary and/or gatekeepers.

❑ Proofread carefully for typos and punctuation.

❑ Assign a date for your follow-up.

COMMENTARY

Never, ever leave the next step to the prospect. Always arrange a definitive time for follow-up. If you call and say, "I'm calling Ms. Garner as promised," and the assistant tells you she's not available, reply, "Well, that happens to all of us. If you have her calendar there, can you tell me when she'll return and perhaps we can pencil in a firm appointment?"

Cold Call Letter

Dear Mr. Conrad:

I've noted in the business press that Acme is having a tough time attracting and retaining talent while trying to hold the line on compensation and benefits. Given the added competition of two major new manufacturing entities within 60 miles, this pressure will undoubtedly increase.

We've specialized in new-hire attraction, retention, evaluation, and development for such firms as Boeing, 3M, Ford, and Exxon. In very brief time frames we:

- Create an allure for your firm in nonmonetary inducements.
- Create a strategy to spread the word, including graduate schools.
- Involve your own employees in recruiting new hires.
- Gain national press coverage positioning you as an employer of choice.

I've enclosed our press kit, which includes references, testimonials, case studies, and our very popular position paper, "Ten Techniques to Immediately Assess Hiring Practices."

I'll call you Friday at 10 a.m. to explore further interest. For your scheduling, I'll be seeing clients within a few minutes of your headquarters on both the 17th and 30th of this month. If you're unavailable on Friday morning, any of the contact points on this letterhead can be used to set up a different time to talk.

Thanks in advance for your consideration. I'm looking forward to meeting you, and I'm confident that we can be of significant assistance in the very short term.

Sincerely,

Alan Weiss
President
Enc.

To download sample templates and checklists, go to www.summitconsulting.com. For more information, visit www.wiley.com/go/summitconsulting.

MEETING PREPARATION

I'm asked all the time the equivalent of "What do I say after I say hello?" It's a shame to go through the work of obtaining a meeting with a buyer but then flubbing the time you have together.

The checklist that follows will help you assemble what you need. But here are some opening gambits to guide you as you initially open your mouth:

"It's very nice to meet you. I know that your time, as mine, is quite squeezed, so perhaps we should agree on the major points that each of us would like to focus on while we're together?" (You begin as peers.)

"Good morning. Your assistant was excellent in setting this meeting up and following through with me, and I wanted to be sure to pass that on to you." (You begin with a nonfawning compliment.)

"It's a pleasure to meet you. I don't believe I've ever been in this complex. It looks new. How long have you been here?" (You begin with a neutral but natural question.)

"Hello, thanks for seeing me. I believe we may have a mutual acquaintance. Jim Brewer at Bosco, Inc., told me that he once worked with you at Allied International. Is that so?" (You begin with something in common.)

MEETING PREPARATION CHECKLIST

- ❏ Prospect company knowledge:
    - ❏ Size of revenues, employees, and number of sites.
    - ❏ Main products, services, and competitors.
    - ❏ History of the firm and place in its industry/profession.
    - ❏ Major recent changes.
    - ❏ Names of key executives.
- ❏ Prospective buyer knowledge:
    - ❏ Accurate name and title.
    - ❏ Years with the company and in current job.
    - ❏ Distinguishing experiences, accolades, accomplishments.

- ❑ Potential fit with your value:
  - ❑ Problem that needs correction.
  - ❑ Decision or plan that needs to be implemented.
  - ❑ Compliance or competitive factors.
  - ❑ Innovation and creativity.
- ❑ Materials and support:
  - ❑ Prospect information, including directions.
  - ❑ What you choose to leave with the prospect.
  - ❑ Notes that you've made on lines of inquiry and pursuit.
  - ❑ Pressed clothing, shined shoes, good pen, car washed.
- ❑ Specific next step:
  - ❑ Another meeting or phone call.
  - ❑ Proposal.

COMMENTARY

You can obtain the background information you need from an Internet search, annual reports, calling the switchboard, talking to the public relations department, networking among colleagues, local news reports, and so forth.

Make sure you look your best. You'll probably park in a visitor's space visible from the building. Rent a car if yours isn't decent. Take an attractive briefcase or portfolio and an expensive-looking pen. People want to interact with successful people. Forget the nonsense about "dressing down." Look as good as you can. (Even if it's a casual workplace, dress in business attire anyway for your first meeting.)

Always have a clear idea of your next step, which you may modify as the discussion continues. But never leave a prospect without an absolute agreement on what happens next and when: phone call, meeting, materials sent and follow-up, formal proposal, and so forth. *One of the biggest mistakes made in consulting sales is leaving the next step to the buyer.* Specify and gain agreement on exactly what will happen next.

NETWORKING

Networking is not "working a room." It is an attempt to find a *few* high-potential prospects or recommenders and develop a relationship.

There are five key aspects to quality networking:

1. *Distance power.* You are better off with people who are strangers than those who know you slightly, because the latter have preconceived perceptions that color their judgment. With the former, you can create a new perception readily.

2. *Unique multipliers.* These are people who may not be buyers, but know scores of people who can help you, so a relationship with them can be leveraged into dozens of relationships.

3. *Nexus people.* These are unique connectors who are insiders with your potential buyers. They can make an immediate introduction, and may be subordinates, assistants, colleagues, family friends, and so on.

4. *Adhesion principle.* What will you do to be memorable? I suggest that *you provide the other person with value,* thereby creating an obligation. That value may be a business contact or a resource, or you may be a nexus person for them.

5. *Contextual connection.* You are both at an event with something in common, be it a charity, school, political party, or social event. Make the best of that immediate common bond.

Networking Checklist

❏ Preparation:

    ❏ Gather information about who will be at the event.

    ❏ Research something about them to provide conversation.

    ❏ Understand the logistics of the event (dinner, cocktails, time frames, etc.).

❏ Active networking:

    ❏ Isolate the individual; don't attempt networking in large group.

- ❏ Keep it brief and gain your objective quickly.
- ❏ Establish some follow-up ("I'll send that information to you").
- ❏ Do not provide anything bulkier than a business card.
- ❏ Follow-up:
  - ❏ Meet your commitment quickly.
  - ❏ Follow up on the receipt and utility of your commitment/ resource.
  - ❏ Provide additional items of value.
  - ❏ Suggest a lunch or meeting after the second helpful gesture.

COMMENTARY

Keep in mind that your immediate objective in networking is a meeting with a buyer. You don't want to make a sales pitch or bore people with how wonderful your approaches are.

By providing value over a brief time span you create an obligation to reciprocate in some fashion. *Networking is a process, not an event.* After the initial networking opportunity you should be investing time over the next two to four weeks in completing this cycle and obtaining your meeting with a buyer (either directly or through referral).

If you network once or twice a month in this manner, you *will* acquire high-quality leads and meetings.

Networking Follow-Up Note

I enjoyed having the opportunity to speak with you at the Charity Awards Dinner, and appreciate your advice about the best ski slopes in Utah since we'll be there in December!

I hope the lead I provided at the Acme Company was of help. Would you like more of these contacts? It's fairly routine for me to find that my clients need help with recruiting issues, which is something my company doesn't handle.

Since we spoke I've discovered that I have business meetings on May 5th and 6th a few blocks from your office. Would breakfast or lunch make sense on either day? I'd like to pick up on several issues we discussed that we had to cut short as the evening's events began.

I'll call at 3 p.m. Thursday, April 29th, to see if your schedule permits a meal or brief meeting. Feel free to call me beforehand at 555-222-1111. Looking forward to renewing our conversation.

ADVERTISING AND LISTINGS

There are a variety of buyer's guides, listings, and resource centers in both hard copy and on the Internet that can make sense for a consultant. Some consultants even advertise in the yellow pages of their local phone books.

While these may not be high-volume sources of qualified leads, they usually are not expensive (some are free), and you need only one good hit to pay for itself forever.

ADVERTISING AND LISTINGS CHECKLIST

- ❑ Choose those sources your potential clients read/refer to.
- ❑ In your ad, focus on client outcomes, not your methodology.
- ❑ Use testimonial blurbs and client lists or examples if possible.
- ❑ Consistently appear for an extended time.
- ❑ Use four-color not black-and-white printing if possible.
- ❑ Use company logo.
- ❑ Evaluate results once a quarter or less, not more often.

COMMENTARY

I've had only one solid lead from an ad I placed beginning 10 years ago in the ASTD Buyer's Guide. But the lead led to a $150,000 project, plus referrals, plus an impressive addition to my client list. The ad cost about $150 a year at the beginning, and costs about $1,000 today.

Ads can also be used as:

- ❏ Copy placed in your press kit.
- ❏ Copy included in your web site.
- ❏ Collateral material that says, "See our advertisement in . . ."
- ❏ Handouts at certain events and exhibitor's booths.

Sample Advertisement

Here is most of my ad that appears in the *Yearbook of Experts*. You can see the complete ad, in color, with my logo and recent news releases, by going to www.yearbook.com, clicking on "Experts," and entering my name as the search item (or entering Summit Consulting Group, Inc.).

PARTICIPANT INFORMATION

Summit Consulting Group, Inc.—Alan Weiss, PhD
East Greenwich, RI, USA

- ▪ Jump to Summit Consulting Group, Inc.—Alan Weiss, PhD
- ▪ Click here to listen to Summit Consulting Group, Inc.—Alan Weiss, Ph.D.
  Or dial 703-243-6572 and enter 3426219 and the pound sign (#).
- ▪ View releases.

CONTACT INFORMATION

Crysta Ames
Office Manager
Summit Consulting Group, Inc.
East Greenwich, RI
Contact Phone: 401-884-2778

- Add Summit Consulting Group, Inc.—Alan Weiss, PhD to your Instant News Wire list.

OTHER EXPERTS ON THESE TOPICS

1. *Behavior* (25 additional experts)
2. *Business Management* (6 additional experts)
3. *Change Management* (12 additional experts)
4. *Consulting* (55 additional experts)
5. *Ethics* (34 additional experts)
6. *Image* (33 additional experts)
7. *Innovation* (16 additional experts)
8. *Motivation* (47 additional experts)
9. *Professional Speaking* (3 additional experts)
10. *Strategy* (19 additional experts)

Click to find more experts on these topics.

BUSINESS AND MANAGEMENT EXPERT ALAN WEISS, PHD

Alan Weiss, PhD, is "one of the most highly regarded independent consultants in the country," according to the *New York Post*. He is the author of *Million Dollar Consulting* (McGraw-Hill, 1992, 1998, 2002), as well as *Making It Work* (on strategy), *Managing for Peak Performance* (on behavior), and *The Unofficial Guide to Power Management*. His books have been major book club selections and translated into German, Spanish, Chinese, and Italian, generating interviews in media around the world.

His newest books are *Life Balance*, *The Ultimate Consultant*, and *Organizational Consulting*. His clients have included Merck, GE, Mercedes-Benz, Hewlett-Packard, GTE, the American Press Institute, the *New York Times*, the American Institute of Architects, *BusinessWeek*, and over 500 other organizations in 54 countries.

Find out why *Success* magazine calls him "an international expert in executive education" and why scores of firms pay top dollar to profit from his advice on productivity and human performance.

FEE SETTING

"How much should I charge?" This is the question I'm asked more than any other. Fee setting is both art and science (as long as you're not charging by the hour, which is neither art nor science, but crazy—your time is *not* your value; your *results* are your value).

Fees should represent a great deal for the buyer—strong return on investment (ROI)—and equitable pay for the consultant. When people ask about my pricing "formula" I respond, "My fees are based on my contribution to the overall results and value you are deriving from this project." Time, of course, is irrelevant, except that the faster you improve the client's condition, the better off you both are. So why use a payment system that is in ethical conflict with that dynamic, since hourly billing only permits you to make money *the longer you take to improve the client's condition*?

Fee Setting Checklist

- ❏ Agree on objectives, metrics, and *value of the project to the buyer*.[3]
- ❏ Provide options with varying degrees of value.
- ❏ Assess total value of the results (profit, repute, teamwork, stress relief, etc.).
- ❏ Assess personal and situational uniqueness in contributing:
  - ❏ Your personal experiences, education, intellectual property, and so on.
  - ❏ Urgency, windows of opportunity, competitive actions under way, and so on.
  - ❏ Past failures to improve, internal inability to handle, need for outsider, and so on.

---

[3]See "Proposals" earlier in this section.

- ❑ Set a range of fees over the options:
  - ❑ Minimum quantitative return to client should be 10:1, probably greater.
  - ❑ Qualitative returns must be dramatic: new brand, improved repute, and so on.
- ❑ Never reduce a fee for an option unless you also reduce value provided.
- ❑ Select advantageous payment terms:
  - ❑ Minimum 50 percent on acceptance.
  - ❑ Request 50 percent balance in 45 days.[4]
  - ❑ Consider 10 percent discount for full payment in advance.

COMMENTARY

In assessing your uniqueness to the project, you're actually asking, "Why me, why now, and why in this manner?" The more uniquely suitable you are (e.g., you're one of the few who can do this or has written a book on the topic; there is a closing window of opportunity; the client tried to solve this internally and failed), the more value you offer and the higher your appropriate fee is. Make sure your projects are noncancelable, and if you allow delays and rescheduling, require that payments be nonetheless due on the original dates, not the new ones.

CLOSING THE SALE

Astoundingly, many consultants are oblivious to the need to close a sale. That is, they begin doing "needs analysis" (almost always totally

---

[4]These optimal billing terms allow you to negotiate from a position of strength (e.g., the balance in 60 days instead of 45). Never agree to a final payment only upon completion. There is nothing inappropriate about accepting full payment within 90 days for a six-month project, for example.

worthless), or interview people, or create methodological approaches, but never gain full agreement with the client buyer, commit it to writing, and officially consummate a deal.

This is why I've advocated proposals that demand agreement on all aspects of the project and require a signature. But in case you don't use them, or you have an existing client with whom they would be superfluous, or you prefer handshakes, here are some guidelines to ensure that you close the business with both your and your buyer's best interests protected.

Read carefully. I can't tell you how many people I've mentored who tell me, "I was sure we had a deal, but now they won't return my calls!" Worse, the consultant has already spent the "sure" money that now is not going to be collected!

Closing the Sale Checklist

- ❑ Specify agreement on these key elements:
  - ❑ Objectives (business outcomes) to be met.
  - ❑ Measures of success (indicators of progress).
  - ❑ Value to the organization.
  - ❑ Accountabilities of you and the client.
  - ❑ Options to go forward.
  - ❑ Fee amount and payment terms.
  - ❑ Timing.
- ❑ Commit to writing in some form:
  - ❑ Proposal.
  - ❑ Summary document prepared by you.
  - ❑ Hard copy in files, not merely electronic.
- ❑ Follow-up items:
  - ❑ Confirm your start date and when you will appear on-site.
  - ❑ Confirm that your initial payment is received.
  - ❑ Confirm internal resources are available and informed, per agreement.

COMMENTARY

Notice that I don't speak about "deliverables," since these are necessary tasks to be completed along the way, but are not terribly important in and of themselves. In other words, it's important to have the internal resources to schedule focus groups and provide refreshments, but the fact that you've facilitated them is not nearly as important as the patterns you analyze that provide recommendations for the new compensation system.

Even a memo sent for file without a signature from the buyer is better than a mere oral agreement. People's memories fade, buyers sometimes change, conditions certainly change, and you can't leave your livelihood to these vagaries of fate.

Self-Development

The material in this section deals with the needs that we all have, as solo practitioners or small firm members, to continually improve our abilities and critically question our methods. It's too simple to fall into the trap of getting better and better at less and less.

READING MATERIALS

Practice management, life balance, and self-development often clash because the same nonrenewable resource is the fuel: time. I've found that self-development is often the one that is sacrificed, which is unfortunate since it's a vital ingredient of the other two.

Reading, particularly, is often placed at the bottom of the priority list or ignored. Just take a look at the pile of magazines and periodicals that have accumulated on your desk or credenza, or think of the ones you discard unread on a regular basis. Some of these may be unnecessary and, therefore, safely ignored. But some may contain important resources and information that, for the solo practitioner, may not be forthcoming from other sources.

My recommendation is that you read on a daily, weekly, and monthly basis specifically for professional development (you should also be reading for pleasure and to pursue hobbies and interests, but total life balance is beyond my purview at the moment). Fortunately, there is a plethora of resources and you need only read a small fraction. Unfortunately, there are also a great many invalid approaches and unsubstantiated claims, even in respected journals and major books.

How to separate the management wheat from the guru chaff?

READING CHECKLIST

- ❏ Daily:
    - ❏ *Wall Street Journal* (or international equivalent, e.g., *Financial Times*).
    - ❏ Hometown newspaper, or local newspaper if traveling.
- ❏ Weekly or biweekly:
    - ❏ *BusinessWeek*.
    - ❏ *Fortune* or *Forbes* (not both).
    - ❏ Local business periodical (e.g., *Crane's Chicago, Providence Business News*).
    - ❏ Sunday edition of the *New York Times* (available almost anywhere).
- ❏ Monthly:
    - ❏ *Consultants News*.
    - ❏ Specialty magazines (e.g., *Inc., Human Resources Executive, Training*).
    - ❏ Two business books.[1]
    - ❏ Newsletters/magazines from trade associations (e.g., *Psychology Today*).

---

[1]These can be biographies, classics, or whatever. As a rule, you can't go wrong reading Peter Drucker's work, no matter when it was written. See the Appendix for a business bibliography.

❑ Quarterly and less frequently:

  ❑ *C2M* (*Consulting to Management*).

  ❑ Annual reports of key clients and prospects.

  ❑ Major listings (e.g., "100 Best Companies for Working Mothers").

COMMENTARY

Note that I've been relatively spare in my recommendations out of respect for your time, pragmatism about discipline, and skepticism about much of what's being published in the field (*Chicken Soup for the Subordinate's 401(k) Investment Soul*).

For example, I've found the *Harvard Business Review* to be largely a waste of time for a sole practitioner consultant, with an occasional article of interest that doesn't justify the time or price, despite the cachet of saying, "I saw this in the *Harvard Business Review*."

Also, I recommend that you keep physical files labeled with key areas of your practice (e.g., "ethics" or "merger and acquisition") and use these for pages you tear out or photocopy from what you read. You can review these files quarterly to see if the material is of help in a book, article, client project, or your web site. Integrate whatever you find relevant, making sure to provide proper attribution. Discard everything else.

ASSOCIATIONS

Trade associations can serve quite a few purposes:

✔ Networking with colleagues for best practices and leads.

✔ Keeping abreast of state-of-the-art developments and calibrating your progress.

✔ Discounted insurance and group coverage.

✔ Annual or more frequent conferences and exhibitions.

✔ Periodicals and reference literature.

✔ Opportunities to speak and to publish.

Examples of trade associations, which can be in your general field (consulting), your specialty (e.g., human resource consulting), or your prospects' and clients' areas (e.g., banking), would be:

✔ Institute of Management Consultants.

✔ Society for Advancement of Consulting.

✔ Society for Human Resource Management.

✔ American Coaching Federation.

✔ American Banking Association.

✔ American Press Institute.

Trade and professional groups can also make huge demands on your time and provide poor guidance and advice, so you must use some discretion. Don't join more than three or four at most, try to take leadership positions where possible, and analyze regularly whether you are getting your money's and time's worth. Remember that just one good idea a month may make it more than worthwhile to belong to a particular association.

ASSOCIATION EVALUATION CHECKLIST

❑ Membership:
    ❑ People who will provide you with "stretch" and growth.
    ❑ Clearly successful practitioners; top people in the field.
    ❑ Diverse—across age, gender, physical ability, and ethnic lines.

❑ Requirements:
    ❑ Based on commitment and ethics, not elitism and rank.
    ❑ Nondiscriminatory.
    ❑ Economically appropriate; no hidden costs later.

❏ Value:

- ❏ Monthly communications and publications provided to members.
- ❏ Access to major people in the field.
- ❏ Opportunity for meetings, chapters, conferences, and so on.
- ❏ Discount for professional services.
- ❏ Recognizable brand and image.

❏ Administration:

- ❏ Run efficiently: letters answered, phone calls answered, problems solved.
- ❏ Administration is less than 10 percent of overall budget.
- ❏ Open and fair opportunities to take visible positions, no in crowd.
- ❏ Allows guest attendance or some other trial membership or attendance.

COMMENTARY

In general, any associations should allow you to come to a meeting as a guest to sample the atmosphere (albeit for a fee) and/or provide a free copy of each publication so that you can assess the value. Certifications are not usually very important because the buying public does not recognize them (as they do, say, a CPA or a PhD). Although useful for self-development if the criteria are tough and enforced, gaining a certificate will seldom help your marketing or public image. Never be lured by initials after your name (Justly Excellent Rigorous Keeper of Yields, or JERKY). You can't deposit them in the bank, and no one is impressed.

REBUTTING OBJECTIONS

The ability to handle objections is an important part of a consultant's self-development because it's a skill that shouldn't be first learned when facing an important prospect, but rather in the calmness of your individual work or practice with colleagues.

Most consultants handle an objection as though it's a new development, a mountain lion that abruptly pounced on the hiking trail a few yards ahead. But the fact is, we've all heard every objection there is. That's right. Here are some examples of the usual suspects:

- ✔ I don't have any budget.
- ✔ The timing isn't right.
- ✔ You're too small; we're looking at larger firms.
- ✔ We'd prefer someone local.
- ✔ We'll probably do this internally.
- ✔ We don't need it.
- ✔ And so on, ad nauseam.

We may not be able to overcome every objection from an intransigent or intractable buyer, *but it's professionally negligent not to at least be prepared for them with rational rebuttal.* Hence, combating objections is an aspect of self-development.

REBUTTING OBJECTIONS CHECKLIST

- ❑ Objections about money:
    - ❑ Demonstrate that the return on investment (ROI) is so great that the investment is mandatory.
    - ❑ Provide options so that differing investments are possible.
    - ❑ Defer the conversation until after you both can agree on objectives.
    - ❑ Demonstrate that there is money; the question is where it is spent.
- ❑ Objections about timing:
    - ❑ Demonstrate that the situation will get worse if not resolved.
    - ❑ Point out that there is no "good time" to intervene and make changes.

❑ Show that time is always available, and that priorities are the real issue.

❑ Suggest a phased approach, but one that begins immediately.

❑ Objections about need:

❑ Buyers know what they want, but not what they need: you create it.

❑ Provide tangible benefits in terms of business outcomes, not theory.

❑ Demonstrate that market perception differs from the prospect's.

❑ Demonstrate a clear competitive edge that will emerge.

❑ Objections about trust:

❑ Provide testimonials, references, third-party endorsements.

❑ Demonstrate that you understand the prospect's industry and organization.

❑ Demonstrate a clear business acumen and consulting depth.

❑ Offer value on the spot.

COMMENTARY

All rational objections (as opposed to "My cousin Louie told me not to spend money this year") fall into the four categories of money, timing, need, or trust. And of those categories, the fourth is the most critical, since the first three tend to be specious and to camouflage the presence of the fourth.

There is always money and time. After all, the lights are on, the cleaning crew is working, the mail is going out; and there are the same number of hours in every day of every week—you can count on it. That means that both money and time investment are matters of *priorities, not availability*. Consequently, don't spend a lot of time on anything other than the fact that your help needs to move up the priority list (as opposed to the terrible response, "Well, when is a good time for me to come back when more resources will be available?").

Objections about need mean that you're not doing your job. As stated earlier, you can raise existing needs, create new needs, or anticipate future needs. It's not up to the prospect to do this; it's up to you, which is why doing your homework is so important.

That leaves us with trust. Providing strong background evidence of your abilities (publishing, references, testimonials, client list, etc.) and strong current evidence of your professionalism (attire, speech, business acumen, immediate value added, etc.) and your future worth (insights, suggestions, provocation, etc.) provides the comfort level that a buyer requires with someone new to eliminate the other three objection categories.

Preparing for, rehearsing, and combating objections is one of the most crucial—and overlooked—aspects of self-development for solo practitioners.

LEARNING FROM SETBACKS

You win some and you lose some. The best baseball hitters are successful about one-third of the time. The best golfers win perhaps one of every 15 tournaments they enter. Abraham Lincoln lost more elections than he won. The finest salespeople probably close about two sales of every 10 legitimate meetings.

The key, of course, is not to make the same mistake twice. Whether you swing at a wild pitch, hit the tee shot into the water, lose the election through poor debating, or lose the sale through lack of preparation about the competition, the idea is to lessen the chances that the same cause will produce the same result the next time.

In other words, a setback is a great improvement opportunity, and one worth mentioning here. In addition, setbacks can provide positive opportunities to exploit the distance you have traveled. After all, you did get as far as a buyer, and were successful in being considered.

Don't shun setbacks. Learn from them. They are an intrinsic part of the work, so we might as well become proficient at dealing with them and capitalizing on lessons learned.

LEARNING FROM SETBACKS CHECKLIST

❏ What was the major cause of lack of success?

    ❏ Ask buyer what you could have done better to garner business.

    ❏ Isolate the key area(s) that you had trouble handling.

    ❏ Was it preventable?[2]

❏ What do you have to do differently in the future?

    ❏ Do more homework on buyer and/or organization and industry.

    ❏ Demonstrate more sophistication in business (e.g., spreadsheets or planning).

    ❏ Improve personal presentation; listen better; provide more accurate handouts.

    ❏ Determine who competition is and create better differentiation.

    ❏ Develop trust and credibility.

    ❏ Follow up and push for urgency.

    ❏ Nothing; it's out of my hands, and best to simply move on.

❏ What can you still recover?

    ❏ Will buyer provide leads with other people in or outside of organization?

    ❏ Can you use experience for publishing, case studies, networking?

    ❏ Can you return in the future? (Never burn bridges.)

    ❏ Can you add names to mailing lists, newsletters, and the like?

    ❏ Are there new technologies/methodologies to begin learning?

---

[2]The buyer suffering the loss of his largest client, creating calamity in his business, is not preventable on your part; the buyer disappointed in your failure to recognize the international impact of your suggested reorganization plan is preventable.

COMMENTARY

There are occasions when the best thing you can do is forget about the loss and move on. "Some coasts," said writer Joseph Epstein, "are set aside for shipwreck." But, more often, we can learn from and even exploit setbacks.

If you've developed a good relationship with the buyer, he or she may be quite willing to give you the names of suppliers, customers, colleagues, and others who might use your help (and thus alleviate their own guilt in not hiring you). You may also discover that there is a type of competition and some approaches in the field that you had better learn about and combat effectively. And you should always be able to stay in contact, since you never want to simply break off a relationship merely because you didn't get business immediately.

Bear in mind that perhaps most of the competition we face is from *internal sources*, not outright competitors. So, understand carefully why the buyer decided to do things within the firm and next time be able to prevent this by pointing out the dangers of doing so (political implications, much more expensive, lack of residual expertise, etc.).

Travel

▀▀▀▀▀▀

This might seem obvious, but learning to travel efficiently and comfortably will enhance your chances for business success. This section contains material that will help you make intelligent decisions about how to turn the road into a home away from home. Some people think checklists about travel are too basic. I don't. You'll spend a lot of your time traveling, and the better you are at taking care of yourself, the more your business dealings will profit.

CLUBS

The clubs that make eminent sense to join are airline clubs, because they offer an oasis of calm in airports where you spend increasing amounts of time both after clearing security and during layovers. Besides refreshments and business centers and help with your scheduling, most of the clubs provide wireless Internet service, meaning you can open your laptop to access e-mail and web sites at high speeds without phone lines or modems.

Since they've become democratic (membership was by invitation only for the most frequent fliers as late as the 1970s until a court case ended the practice), even the airline clubs can become crowded, and they've responded by raising their prices dramatically. Nevertheless, they are bargains and—check with your accountant—are often a legitimate business expense. (Most have conference rooms for meetings, meaning you can fly in, not worry about reentering security, have your meeting, and depart again on the same day.)

Other types of clubs can be useful for meetings in other cities if they have affiliation agreements. For example, the University Club has outposts in more than 20 cities and affiliations in another dozen, some overseas. Besides representing a high-quality place to take someone to lunch (no money is accepted—you simply sign the voucher), they frequently provide space to make phone calls and work while you're between appointments, and many have exercise rooms. Other clubs offer shared access to secretaries, photocopiers, and other office amenities for an annual subscription.

Finally, a health club with national outlets can be important for working out while traveling, though most hotels have their own facilities.

CLUBS CHECKLIST

- ❑ Do you own or can you obtain a multiclub card? American Express and others offer automatic membership to several clubs.[1]
- ❑ Obtain memberships to the airlines you most often fly:
    - ❑ Two national carriers and one regional carrier, as appropriate.
    - ❑ Check for reciprocal agreements with other airlines, especially international.
    - ❑ Single card, not spouse.
    - ❑ You can use airline frequent-flier points to purchase if you prefer.
    - ❑ Check for conference rooms, wireless Internet, long hours of operation.

---

[1]For example, an American Express Platinum Card will get you into Northwest Airlines' and Continental Airlines' air clubs, as well as automatic membership in the Hertz Corporation's rental car gold program.

❑ Private clubs:

  ❑ Represented in towns you most frequently visit.

  ❑ Central billing agreement.

  ❑ Acceptable dress code (usually require jacket and tie for men).

  ❑ Serve lunch and dinner (some will serve breakfast).

  ❑ Atmosphere conducive for client meetings.

  ❑ Health club and amenities.

  ❑ International representation/affiliations.

❑ Business clubs:

  ❑ Business services (secretary, fax, private phones, Internet, etc.).

  ❑ Represented in towns you most frequently visit.

  ❑ Meeting rooms.

  ❑ Centrally located.

COMMENTARY

Even if you spend as much as $2,500 a year on private clubs of one sort or another, it's probably a great investment based on the expense and the wear and tear they will save you. In airports, for example, they are of immense help when flights are delayed or canceled or you must make a last-minute change. In cities, during inclement weather, a club and a limo service can be lifesavers.

Even in your hometown, if you work out of your home, a club gives you the option of meeting clients and prospects in a professional atmosphere as well as dining in relative privacy for business conversations. Many offer private rooms exactly for that purpose.

Some airline clubs offer reciprocity domestically (join Northwest Airlines and you can use Continental Airlines' President's Club on the same day as your flight), or join American and you can use British Air Clubs overseas (these affiliations sometimes change, but you get the idea).

As a solo practitioner, the traveling life is probably going to capture you, so you might as well make it a good life while you're at it.

TRANSPORTATION AND LODGING

The way you perform at meetings, seminars, interviews, and the like is often a factor of how you arrived there! Making it to a focus group at the last minute or being late for a meeting with the buyer will not be conducive to your best performance in either case.

Transportation is often an afterthought, but I'm convinced that it plays a subliminal yet vital part in how prepared, refreshed, confident, and flexible you are. You want your mind on the sale, the delivery, the discussion, and so on, not on whether you'll make a connection, get drenched, or be uncomfortable.

By codifying your travel (and alerting your travel agent to your needs and routine), you'll go a long way toward improving your overall mental health and business effectiveness.

So, don't laugh, but here are some vital considerations that have helped me enormously.

TRANSPORTATION AND LODGING CHECKLIST

- ❏ Air:
    - ❏ Utilize as few carriers as possible to maximize frequent-flier miles/service.
    - ❏ Try to fly first class whenever you can.[2]
    - ❏ Join key air clubs.
    - ❏ Always have backup flights in mind.

---

[2] I flew first class from the first day I opened the door with no business. Among other advantages: first on and off the plane; better legroom; room for even large laptop computers; free drinks; usually decent food; strong ticket that is easy to exchange, refund, or gain priority for rescheduling; shorter, special check-in lines; often special, shorter security lines; special offers extended; amenity package internationally. Need I say more?

❑ Purchase power cord converter for laptop power supply at seat.

❑ Arrive early for security with work/reading to do during wait for plane.

❑ Bring only carry-on bag(s) for brief trips; send luggage ahead for longer trips.[3]

❑ Surface, local:

    ❑ Consider limos rather than taxis; join a national group, such as Carey Limousine.

    ❑ Subways and light rail tend to be highly safe, fast, and reliable.

❑ Surface, distant:

    ❑ Join the highest-level rental car program you can for the amenities.

    ❑ Seek global positioning systems in every rental car.

    ❑ If your normal insurance applies, never accept the insurance offered.

    ❑ Master all controls before leaving the lot.

    ❑ Use MapQuest or another online directions system before you leave home.

    ❑ Auto clubs will also help you with routing.

❑ Phone:

    ❑ Make sure your cell phone will work where you are headed.[4]

    ❑ Ensure that your cell phone is fully charged before the trip; carry a spare charged battery.

---

[3]The check luggage lines are the longest and slowest in the airports. If you're going to spend a week somewhere, you can FedEx your luggage to meet you upon your arrival. I do this on vacations, as well.

[4]You can easily rent cell phones locally and internationally, or acquire a cell phone that will work in most countries.

❑ If a prolonged trip, bring a car charger for the phone as well as a charger that you can plug in at the hotel.

❑ Preprogram all vital numbers, including those of clients, prospects, travel agent, and so on.

❑ Hotel:

  ❑ Join all frequent-guest programs (almost all are free and apply to airlines).

  ❑ Always request a better room and upgrade (granted about half the time).

  ❑ Stay only where rooms have Ethernet or wireless Internet access.

  ❑ Use cell phone or phone credit card, not hotel service, for calls.

  ❑ If possible, choose hotels with concierge to help with plans, emergencies.

  ❑ Consider staying on the concierge floor for additional amenities and comfort.

COMMENTARY

Not only are taxis dirty, noisy, and unsafe, but also the drivers in major cities increasingly have no idea where things are and spend their time talking on their cell phones. A limo is barely more expensive and is clean and classy; allows you to make phone calls; and will pick you up at airports, train stations, clients, and so on. If you have several stops within one city, consider hiring the limo for several hours. Especially in inclement weather, this is well worth the investment.

Even midrange hotels such as those of Marriott International and Hyatt Corporation generally have concierges, who can help you with local transportation, meals, business needs, even finding a tie or blouse to replace the one that you spilled marinara sauce on. Combining hotel, credit card, and airline frequent-travel points can quickly get you free tickets and free accommodations, very useful when you are marketing and spending your own money. Just being a member of most hotel frequent-stay programs will get you an upgraded room, special check-in line, continental breakfast, and other amenities.

If you travel a lot, use a cell phone plan with free roaming and stop worrying about it. Make sure your phone and laptop stay charged. Never, ever check these items on an airplane.

Don't be penny wise and pound foolish. A Ritz-Carlton, for example, is a top hotel that seems very expensive. But if you stay on the concierge floor, you can, literally, have three (or more) free meals a day there, hold a business meeting, and get your suit pressed. Think about the big picture.

ROAD WARRIOR SUPPORT

I've alluded to some of the items that are vital on the road, but here is a useful master list of the full panoply.

You can add and adjust to your heart's content, but heed three rules of thumb:

1. You are not a pack animal.
2. Try as you might, you can't prepare for every remote contingency.
3. This is not a competition. (I love watching people with status ultrathin cell phones who can't even hold them comfortably.)

ROAD WARRIOR SUPPORT CHECKLIST

❑ Cell phone:
  ❑ Chargers and/or spare batteries.
  ❑ Preprogrammed with all key numbers.
  ❑ Ensure it will work where you are traveling.

- ❏ Laptop computer:
    - ❏ Power conversion cord for airplanes that provide power at seats.
    - ❏ Wireless equipped (airport card) for use in airports, hotels, and so on.
    - ❏ Carries main files and duplications from office computer.
- ❏ Separate toiletries kit: entire kit travels with you, no transfer back and forth from bathroom cabinet to luggage.
- ❏ Identification:
    - ❏ Passport, with photocopy of ID page carried in safe, separate spot.
    - ❏ Driver's license.
    - ❏ Numbers of credit card companies (in case of loss or theft).
- ❏ Travel alarm clock with light.
- ❏ Client and prospect background and records.
- ❏ Travel itinerary with all phone numbers and confirmations.
- ❏ Briefcase that can accommodate computer (not a computer tote bag).
- ❏ Overnight carry-on bag that can accommodate at least one suit, wrinkle-free.
- ❏ Extra prescriptions for glasses and medications, in case of loss.
- ❏ Club membership cards and account numbers.
- ❏ Extra work or recreational reading/games in case of delays, long waits.
- ❏ Photos of family.
- ❏ List of special family occasions for shopping, phone calls, cards.
- ❏ FedEx or courier account number and extra air bills for emergency shipping.
- ❏ Extra marketing literature/brochures for unexpected opportunities.

- ❑ *Official Airline Guide* (pocket edition) for quick changes of flight plans.
- ❑ Workout and exercise clothes.
- ❑ Small dictation recorder if you prefer this to notes.
- ❑ Personal digital assistant and/or Filofax or similar calendar system.
- ❑ Prepare for emergencies:
  - ❑ Have all key phone numbers in your cell phone and computer.
  - ❑ Have a physical list in case those items are stolen.
  - ❑ Carry with you all prescriptions and medical notification/insurance cards.
  - ❑ Always let family members know your locations and contact points.
  - ❑ Call home twice a day.
  - ❑ Carry with you business letterhead and envelopes/labels.[5]
  - ❑ Create relationship with secretarial service at home.

COMMENTARY

Try to use a travel agent to whom you provide all of your business you can, even if you tend to use online reservation services. That agent will be loyal to you and always look for the best deals. (One saved me $4,000 on a cruise.) Also, when you're stuck in an airport with delays, it's easier to call your travel agent than to try to call a dozen airlines to make alternative arrangements. One speed dial button on your cell phone and you're in business, and I've often done that to catch an earlier flight while actually driving to the airport to return home.

---

[5]Included in my emergencies would be a client who desperately needs something from you or a prospect who urgently wants a proposal while you're not due back in the office for a week.

Carry the normal array of remedies: aspirin, eyedrops, antacid pills, Band-Aids, and the like. Some people like to have a small flashlight in case of power failure or if they have to find something that rolled under the furniture. On each trip I like to stay at the same hotels, use the same limo companies, and so forth. People get to know you and almost any request will be accommodated, even if it's "out of policy."

One final comment: Some people spend an inordinate amount of their energy trying to maneuver for upgrades in airlines and hotels. If they spent that same amount of energy in their business, they might be successful enough to actually afford the junior suites and first class cabin. Invest in your travel and well-being no less than you'd invest in your portfolio. You have to spend money to make money.

Project Delivery

This section deals with the issues and items you need in delivering your services. Readers are engaged in a plethora of consulting and professional services offerings, and it's not my intent to provide content advice on your specialties. However, there are general delivery *processes* that apply to all of us. This section assumes the sale aspect is completed and implementation is beginning.

SPONSORS

Sometimes included as stakeholders, these are actually the relatively few people who can make or break implementation. I prefer to think of them as "champions."

Sponsors are the formal and informal leaders of an organization to whom people look to understand commitment, urgency, direction, and so forth. Consequently, they may be hierarchical (president, general manager); expert (research scientist, top salesperson); structural (union leader, auditor); or charismatic (popular, well-known).

If you co-opt the sponsors as early as possible, your project will tend to be frictionless. If you co-opt some while ignoring others, you may create political camps. If you ignore sponsors altogether, you're doomed. You may have the sale and the initial deposit in the bank, but the chances for success and renewal business (and, perhaps, even subsequent fees for the current project) are remote.

There are *always* sponsors. The buyer will *always* know who they are, unless the buyer was beamed down that morning from a mother ship. Find out who they are before you begin doing anything else. Then make a plan to influence, cajole, and romance them.

SPONSOR CHECKLIST

- ❑ Preproject agreement:
    - ❑ Find out who the sponsors are from questioning, reading, observing, and so on.
    - ❑ Try to meet and get acquainted early.
- ❑ During project acceptance:
    - ❑ Formally contact and request inputs, opinions, advice.
    - ❑ Form a steering group or oversight team utilizing sponsors.
    - ❑ Arrange for periodic meetings and more frequent phone and mail contact.
- ❑ During project delivery:
    - ❑ Actively engage sponsors and seek opinions about progress.
    - ❑ Provide credit for their assistance to sponsors' superiors.
    - ❑ Publicize sponsors' involvement and communicate it to organization.
- ❑ Postdelivery:
    - ❑ Thank sponsors publicly and privately.
    - ❑ Ask sponsors for testimonials for your work.
    - ❑ Ask sponsors for referrals within or outside of organization.
    - ❑ Add to contact lists, and stay in touch frequently.

COMMENTARY

Sponsors can be superb supporters and referral sources. Never take sides if you find yourself embroiled in a political tug-of-war. Remain neutral and demonstrate to both sides that they are better off supporting your project than opposing it. Be on the alert for missed sponsors as the project develops, expands, or changes.

Perception is everything. A sponsor's presence at a debriefing may be sufficient to support your position even though the sponsor's active support beyond that may be negligible. Understand that you're managing a virtual team with these people, and you have to establish that "we all win or all lose" and there are no individual wins and losses.

In a worst-case scenario, if a key sponsor is in outright opposition, gather tangible evidence of what was said or done, and go to your buyer with the facts. Ask your ultimate sponsor, the buyer, to intercede by changing the sponsor's behavior or removing the obstruction from the path of the project.

INTERVIEWS

Inevitably, we wind up interviewing client employees (and/or customers, vendors, partners, etc.) as part of our projects. Most interviews are terribly labor-intensive, because they are too long and unstructured. Also, if you are employing subcontractors for interviews, you want to be certain that they use a uniform process and preparation to maximize quality.

This interview checklist can be used for any type of interview and any person. It will ensure your own consistency and increase the comfort level and, hence, responsiveness of the subject.

INTERVIEW CHECKLIST

❑ Preparatory work:

❑ Arrange for private, windowless (interior) room, with private approach.

❑ Ensure time, duration, and location are communicated to participants.

❑ Reconfirm with each participant the day before. (This is something a client administrator should do.)

❑ Arrange for water, coffee, soft drinks in interview room as appropriate.

❑ Prepare your questions and test with people to gauge effectiveness.

❑ Schedule interviews for 30 minutes, planning to use 20.

❑ Allow 15 minutes between interviews.

❑ If using a laptop, ensure outlet or battery sufficiency.

❑ During interview:

 ❑ Greet participant at door and thank him or her for coming.

 ❑ Verify the participant's name and position, if needed for survey work.

 ❑ Provide ground rules:

 Confidentiality.

 Note taking is only for your recording of patterns of response.

 About 20 minutes in length.

 Participant should feel free to elaborate on or refuse to answer a question.

 Reason for interview and use of data collected.

 ❑ Go through your list, and ask follow-up questions as responses dictate.

 ❑ Allow responses to be complete; try never to interrupt.

 ❑ Final question should be, "What else, if anything, would you like to add?"

 ❑ Summarize what you heard for benefit of participant and possible correction.

 ❑ Thank participant and escort to door.

❑ Postinterview:

    ❑ Review notes for legibility.

    ❑ Review any points raised to include in future questions.

    ❑ Prepare for next interview.

COMMENTARY

Most interviews become circular after about 20 minutes. A structured, tested set of interview questions should obtain everything you need within that time. Obviously, for political or cultural reasons (interviewing senior offices, union leaders, etc.) you may want to extend the time and allow people to talk for longer periods.

Don't be afraid to say, "Excuse me—I'm sorry to interrupt, but you said something fascinating that I want to follow up," which enables you to end a dreary monologue and return to a key point with all due courtesy.

Interviews are most valuable when patterns and trends emerge, especially when combined with focus groups, surveys, and observation. Further, they are very effective when early responses are built into later questions in order to test their validity (e.g., "Some of your colleagues have reported that they haven't received performance evaluations in more than a year. Is that your understanding and/or experience as well?").

Even some one-off comments in interviews can be very important—for example, the single person from the warehouse who reports, "I would like to answer that, but my attention has been diverted lately by all the theft."

FOCUS GROUPS

Focus groups are sessions run with employees, customers, vendors, or others to obtain opinions, information, and advice about an organization's products, services, and/or relationships. They are ideally run by a third party to remove any political interest or built-in bias of company personnel.

These are one of the easiest yet most important capabilities for a consultant. If facilitated correctly, focus groups provide invaluable information for the client and offer the consultant the opportunity to engage in targeted, high-value analysis and recommendations—often enabling additional project work.

However, a poorly run focus group—or a series of focus groups that do not deliver useful information—will end your career with that client. Ironically, one of the worst things you can do is overprepare for them, since the facilitation job actually involves gentle guidance and not specific direction.

FOCUS GROUP CHECKLIST

❑ Objectives:
   ❑ Information and analysis sought is agreed upon with buyer.
   ❑ Focus group audience is specified and agreed upon as appropriate.
   ❑ Output and deliverables are clear (e.g., report, presentation, etc.).
❑ Administration:
   ❑ Accountability for administration is established (client or consultant).
   ❑ Scheduling, follow-up, backup attendees are managed.
   ❑ Room, refreshments, directions, timing are conveyed and managed.
   ❑ Cover letter is provided:
   Confidential session.
   Voluntary or mandatory.
   Directions to session, duration, attire.
   Topic and expectations.
   ❑ Arrange for a windowless room with private access if possible.

❑ Preparation:

    ❑ Establish a dozen major questions to stimulate discussion.

    ❑ Establish six follow-up questions for each major question.

    ❑ Use a laptop for notes if at all possible, otherwise diligently write.

    ❑ Reconfirm all arrangements the day before with your client contact.

    ❑ Dress the way attendees will be dressed.

    ❑ Arrive at least 30 minutes early.

❑ Facilitation:

    ❑ Start on time.

    ❑ Welcome participants and introduce yourself.

    ❑ Explain reason for note taking and that no names will be attached to comments.

    ❑ Explain that anyone may speak at any time, but respect and civility are paramount.

    ❑ Request that confidentiality regarding discussions be honored.

    ❑ Reemphasize stopping time.

    ❑ Encourage everyone to speak; be comfortable waiting out silences.

    ❑ Never take sides; ask, "How do the rest of you feel about that?"

    ❑ Summarize at the conclusion to demonstrate accuracy of your notes.

    ❑ Thank everyone and tell them what the next steps are.

COMMENTARY

With rare exceptions, it's preferable not to have direct superior/subordinate relationships and not to involve more than two or three levels of the organization's hierarchy in any one group. I've found that a focus group can be highly effective in as little as an hour's time, and that two hours is generally the outer limit before the conversations become circular and people become preoccupied about personal issues or work they are missing. The smallest group that makes sense to me, allowing for proper dynamics, a feeling of confidentiality, and the inevitable people who will not contribute much at all, is 12. The largest that is comfortably manageable is a group of 25. Make sure that you have a system to replace last-minute cancellations, and also to reconfirm with everyone by phone the day before.

If you're doing multiple groups in one day, allow yourself at least a half-hour between groups to think about what you've heard, adjust your questions, and refresh yourself. (I've done as many as four in a day.)

It's best if you can work with the client to disseminate the results of the focus groups, explaining patterns of feedback, major issues, and so on. Either you or the client can do this, at a meeting or in writing. I've found it's more effective for the consultant to do it, preferably at a series of company meetings. This way, people are assured that their feedback was accurately conveyed and they will be more inclined to participate in the future. Also, management is placed in a position of accountability to both acknowledge and act on the feedback.

Template for Focus Group Rules

1. The discussion is confidential. While I can only request that each of you observe the confidential nature of the discussion, I can guarantee to you that I will never identify you in any way, and I will eliminate any references you make that may accidentally identify you (e.g., the youngest woman working in group claims).
2. I'll ask some questions that any of you may answer at any time. I'll also ask some follow-up questions to your responses. Indicate your willingness to contribute by raising a hand and I will acknowledge everyone who does so.

3. Note that there are no name tents or attendance lists. Don't identify yourself when you speak.

4. The computer (or notepad) is simply for me to record accurately your comments. I'll read these back to you before we adjourn so that you can assess whether I've correctly captured your opinions and comments. There are no other recording devices of any kind in this room.

5. We will stop when we've exhausted the topic. That will probably be between 60 and 90 minutes from now. We will not go beyond 90 minutes.

6. Refreshments are available in the back of the room whenever you would like to take some.

7. Please respect all opinions. If you disagree, do so with facts and not with blame or ill feelings. The more examples you can use to support your comments, the better.

8. If I don't hear from some of you I may call on you. You have the option of responding or telling me you'd rather not, which is fine. But I want to make sure you have the opportunity to be heard while we're together.

9. As a result of these sessions—and this is the seventh of 10—I will provide a report directly to your CEO, which will then be shared—unedited—with all employees.

ON-SITE OBSERVATIONS

As a consultant, it helps to be somewhat skeptical and not believe everything you are told, even by the buyer. That doesn't necessarily mean that you believe you are being lied to, but rather that client executives may be seeing things through a tinted lens, or may not be told the truth by subordinates who feel they are protecting their bosses from unpleasant news, a quite common phenomenon.

Consequently, it makes sense to convince yourself and to validate what the client believes or doesn't believe by observing behavior and looking for evidence. That means wandering around and watching what's happening without creating your own "Hawthorne Effect."[1]

You may be observing formally—that is, you've specified that you're going to be wandering around the claims department observing how often the phones go unanswered or the way people communicate or whether managers' doors are open. However, the best observation is often informally, when you are on your way to a meeting, conducting interviews, or chatting with managers, and you notice things around you. In those instances, there is the least probability that anyone has been informed or is even aware of your observation, minimizing the Hawthorne Effect, and you are most probably seeing work life as it actually transpires in that area.

Observations are also best when done comprehensively. I've found myself in areas of the organization—warehouses, purchasing departments, remote field offices—where many of the executives haven't been for years (or ever) and thereby have much better knowledge of their organization's actual behavior than they do.

ON-SITE OBSERVATION CHECKLIST

- ❑ What to observe:
  - ❑ Numbers of people at their desks or workstations over time.
  - ❑ Phones being personally answered.
  - ❑ Condition of the workplace; orderliness or disorder.
  - ❑ Demeanor of employees: smiling, hostile, speaking in the open or furtively.

[1]The "Hawthorne Effect" refers to a famous study conducted at a plant in Hawthorne, New Jersey, that found that mere attention to employees affected performance. In this case, turning the lights up resulted in higher levels of production, but so did turning the lights down. The research has been debunked because of poor controls for the experiment, but the term remains to indicate that consultants may actually influence behavior merely by dint of watching.

To download sample templates and checklists, go to www.summitconsulting.com. For more information, visit www.wiley.com/go/summitconsulting.

- ❑ Management presence or lack of presence; open or shut doors of individuals.
- ❑ People present prior to starting time, over lunch, and after ending time.
- ❑ Arguing or friendly kidding and pranks.
- ❑ Employee personalization of desk space, cubicles, offices.
- ❑ Signs and reminders—employee activities, parties, communal notices.
- ❑ Flexibility and diversity versus regimen and homogeneity.
- ❑ Why observe and how to analyze:
  - ❑ Watch for overarching patterns, not one-off behaviors.
  - ❑ Determine whether this is a friendly, impersonal, or hostile workplace.
  - ❑ Determine whether collegial or hierarchical boundaries most apply.
  - ❑ Understand priority of customer service and responsiveness.
  - ❑ Watch for voluntary work versus strictly nine-to-five mentalities.
  - ❑ Determine if workplace is team-centered or individually competitive.
  - ❑ Determine whether it is a highly productive or highly wasteful environment.
  - ❑ Assess whether resources are present to do the job properly.
  - ❑ Assess whether management and oversight are apparent.
- ❑ What to do with findings:
  - ❑ Document with specific observations supporting claims/ findings.
  - ❑ Suggest further aspects of project or additional work as needed.
  - ❑ Adjust your project work to accommodate actual work culture.

COMMENTARY

There is no surer way to be unsuccessful than to put your credence in a management ukase such as, "Everyone is a team player here," or "People just don't care and are totally out for themselves." You must validate such statements or you may be employing the right tools for the wrong job.

Culture is simply the set of beliefs that governs behavior. By watching behavior you'll know what people believe: that you can either trust management or not; customers are either important or pains in the neck; the company either values diversity or merely pays it lip service; people either go the extra mile or try to take advantage.

If you combine interventions such as surveys, interviews, focus groups, and personal observations, the patterns that emerge will be highly valid and critical for both the education of your client and your own decisions about how to most effectively proceed. Don't kid yourself—people in organizations do not believe what they read and hear. They believe only what they *see*.

So should you.

COACHING

Formally or informally, consultants are frequently coaching their clients. In fact, an entire coaching industry has recently arisen, complete with "universities" and "accreditations." But coaching isn't rocket science, and most of us have been doing it quite naturally for a long time.

That's not to say that there isn't a methodology to coaching and key quality issues. An individual is coached with the explicit objective of improvement in some area, perhaps as minor as facilitating a meeting or as major as reducing anger. That means there should be clear developmental objectives, checkpoints, reviews, and so on. Other topics in this section, such as on-site observations, debriefings, and reports, will all help in this regard.

COACHING CHECKLIST

- ❑ Preparation:
  - ❑ Who is the client—coaching subject or subject's superior?[2]
  - ❑ Establish objectives for improvement.
  - ❑ Establish metrics for improvement progress assessment.
  - ❑ Establish rules of engagement (see template).
- ❑ Active coaching:
  - ❑ Observe in a variety of contexts.
  - ❑ Provide timely, private feedback.
  - ❑ Invite coaching subject's own assessment and critique.
  - ❑ Adjust plans for next steps and repeat process.
  - ❑ Always provide specific examples, not generalities.
  - ❑ Record and document your findings and the subject's reactions.
- ❑ Postcoaching:
  - ❑ Provide for some continuing access to create transition period.
  - ❑ Submit final report to client if client is not subject.

COMMENTARY

Coaching durations vary, depending on the nature of the improvement required and the opportunities for development. Generally, if someone is being coached while in the same position with the same responsibilities for longer than 90 days, there is the danger that the coaching relationship has changed to one of reliance on the coach as a partner.

Coaching should be undertaken with project fees, never with hourly fees, which immediately create a conflict between a rapid improvement and the consultant's amount of remuneration. Also, you don't want to be in a position where the client is making an investment

---

[2]This is important to determine with whom to share feedback, what is confidential and what is not, and so forth.

decision (purchase more of your time) when concerns come up, rather than simply contacting you immediately for assistance.

Coaching Rules of Engagement Template

Developmental goals: What are our specific improvement objectives? How will we know we're reaching them? What will be the value to you and to the organization of achieving them?

Strategic
1. How much access will be provided and by what means?
2. Is there total candor on both sides?
3. Is this confidential or to be reported to a third party?
4. What are acceptable time frames for returning phone calls and e-mail?
5. What is the grievance procedure, if either of us is unfair or violates the rules?
6. What about emergencies (e.g., personal issues)?
7. What are our time frames?
8. How will the feedback take place and in what form?

Tactics
1. Periodic private interviews, especially before and after certain events.
2. Shadowing during all or parts of a day.
3. Observing selected events.
4. Interviews with others with whom you interact (360˚).
5. Interviews with customers.
6. Pre- and post-tests you employ or design.
7. Exercises (e.g., anger control, stress reduction, etc.).
8. Involvement of relevant others.
9. Subject's own ongoing self-assessment.

Paradigms
1. Focus exclusively on observed behavior and evidence.
2. Remove emotionally laden language (e.g., "Why are you so immature?").

3. Provide clear, pragmatic, and immediate improvement techniques.
4. Build on and exploit strengths; don't merely correct weaknesses.
5. Both confront and comfort.
6. Use project fees so that your time isn't an investment decision.
7. Walk your own talk and model the behavior.
8. *Never* take political sides—you're a coach, not an advocate.
9. Create a clear disengagement point.
10. Allow for continuing self-development.
11. Create a final report.

DEBRIEFINGS

You will be debriefing clients both formally and informally. That means you will be providing an update on progress or a final report on results and next steps to your buyer and, perhaps, assorted others.

Debriefings can be single occurrences, one-on-one, or multiple appearances before large groups of people (e.g., the client wants the employees to hear the results directly from the consultant to assure them that no spin-doctoring has occurred).

These sessions are important for four reasons:

1. They are interactive events with the buyer.

2. They are influential in how you are perceived.

3. They can lead easily to additional business.

4. They establish what should happen next to ensure success.

Never wing it. Nor do you have to prepare for a sound-and-light show. Determine through conversations with the buyer what format and time frame are best, and adjust accordingly. *Reports are fine if they are required, but they are never as effective as you, in person, providing valuable information and actions for your client.* Never allow a report to serve as your sole debriefing technique.

DEBRIEFING CHECKLIST

- ❑ Create timing and expectations for formal sessions:
    - ❑ Weekly or monthly during project, and at conclusion.
    - ❑ Phone and e-mail may substitute for in-person meeting on occasion.
    - ❑ Establish durations and desired format, as well as audience.
- ❑ Plan informal debriefings when conversing with buyer or at other opportune moments.
- ❑ Content needs:
    - ❑ Objectives of project.
    - ❑ Measures of success and actual progress to date against them.
    - ❑ Current value already being derived.
    - ❑ Contemporary accomplishments and setbacks.
    - ❑ Hard evidence and observed behavior, not conjecture.
    - ❑ Documents and handouts as appropriate.
    - ❑ Steps for fine-tuning and changing protocols, if needed.
    - ❑ Any additional resource needs that have developed.
- ❑ Delivery needs:
    - ❑ Notes with any relevant handouts.
    - ❑ Visuals as needed: easel sheets, overhead slides, PowerPoint, and so on.
    - ❑ Privacy.
    - ❑ Anticipated questions and responses rehearsed.
    - ❑ Documentation of all material used in debriefings, even in-formal ones.

COMMENTARY

The buyer *must* be the key object of any debriefing. Others may be added as the buyer sees fit. If there are confidential or sensitive mat-

To download sample templates and checklists, go to www.summitconsulting.com. For more information, visit www.wiley.com/go/summitconsulting.

ters, apprise the buyer in advance so that the decision about whom else to involve can be made with that perspective.

Put "victories" and "defeats" in perspective—too many consultants don't debrief unless they have a problem to report. Request help from the buyer as needed (e.g., to influence a key sponsor who has not been cooperative). This is not a test of your abilities, nor is it a commentary on them. Remember, the buyer and you are partners, not superior and subordinate.

If geography or schedules make personal debriefing difficult, then use an uninterrupted conference call, not a cell phone conversation. Document everything you say and provide in case someone says at a later date, "You never told us about that problem."

REPORTS

These are the bane of most consultants' existence, and rightfully so. I stopped doing almost all reports many years ago when I discovered that clients simply lost them on dusty shelves, and that debriefings were far more valuable.

Nonetheless, there are times when a report is called for or demanded by a client and can't be realistically refused. In that case, it's important to provide something of maximum utility to the buyer while avoiding undue labor intensity on your part.

Even when lengthy reports are required for some reason (e.g., background information, statistics on data gathered, comparisons of alternative courses of action, risk analysis, etc.), an executive summary at the beginning will make things a lot more pragmatic and acceptable.

(*Note:* Many consultants position the report as a deliverable and an outcome of the project, which is why they are paid so little. A report, in and of itself, is not intrinsically of high value. That's why avoiding reports or minimizing them has only positive consequences. Your fee is based on value, which in turn is based on business results, not tasks or deliverables.)

REPORT CHECKLIST

- ❏ Timing and expectations: When is the report due and in what preferred format? Don't guess.
- ❏ Content needs:
  - ❏ Objectives of project.
  - ❏ Measures of success and final results.
  - ❏ Value being delivered, not on an annualized basis.
  - ❏ Hard evidence and observed behavior supporting results, not conjecture.
  - ❏ Documents and handouts as appropriate, with commensurate detail/sources.
  - ❏ Specific next steps required to preserve momentum and results.
- ❏ Delivery and environmental needs:
  - ❏ Appropriate for format: slides, hard copy document, and so on.
  - ❏ Confidentiality marked on report and preserved in environment.
  - ❏ Clear distinction between work product and your own intellectual property.[3]
  - ❏ Multiple media (e.g., hard copy of slides, electronic version of text).
  - ❏ Include your name prominently in several places (cover, cover sheet, end).
  - ❏ Hard copy bound or placed in high-quality binder; consider color, client logo.

---

[3]Anything you've inserted from your prior knowledge base, such as a strategy model, remains your proprietary work. Anything you've developed specifically for this client with client resources (e.g., a field compensation system) is work product owned by the client.

To download sample templates and checklists, go to www.summitconsulting.com. For more information, visit www.wiley.com/go/summitconsulting.

COMMENTARY

Ensure that someone picking up this report at a later date (e.g., the buyer's replacement) will clearly know that you produced it and how to reach you. Separate what the client owns as work product from what you already own by placing your copyright or trademark as appropriate on your personal intellectual property within the report.

As long as this physical embodiment of the project has been requested, make it as professional and attractive as possible. Don't stint on the report appearance after a $50,000 project. If electronic formats are requested, use attachments, not embedded e-mail, since the latter will tend to scramble formatting and symbols. However, it's best to have a physical copy at least as backup in any case, well assembled and on the best-quality paper.

Maintain copies of such reports for at least five years *after* your last engagement with a client.

Client Satisfaction Survey Template

Thank you for participating in this quick survey to test our responsiveness and effectiveness for your organization. Simply hit "Reply" and respond to the following questions either by pasting them in or merely by using the number. We would appreciate your response prior to June 15. The survey takes about seven minutes.

1. How would you describe our work with you? Please check one box:
   ❑ Better than other providers.
   ❑ About the same as other providers.
   ❑ Not as good as other providers.
2. Please tell us why you responded as you did to question 1. Specific examples are always helpful.

_____

_____

3. What is our response time to your needs? Please check one box:
   - ❑ Excellent, well within my expectations.
   - ❑ Erratic, sometimes better than others.
   - ❑ Poor, much slower than I'd prefer.

4. What one thing could we do to better serve you?

   _____

5. Are there any outstanding problems at the moment for which you would like an immediate visit or phone call?
   - ❑ Yes, please ❑ call or ❑ schedule a visit.
   - ❑ No.

6. What has been your experience in working with us compared to your original expectations? Please check one box:
   - ❑ Exceeded my expectations.
   - ❑ Met my expectations.
   - ❑ Failed to meet my expectations.

7. Please tell us why you responded as you did to question 6.

   _____

   _____

8. Please feel free to add any comments or observations, and/or to raise issues we haven't addressed in questions 1 through 7. Thanks very much for your participation!

   _____

   _____

Forms

This section deals with the diversity and content of the repeating forms you will probably need in your practice, from invoices to client follow-up, and from expense reporting to subcontracting agreements. If you can create your own "library" of these forms—and feel free to use mine—then your workload will be dramatically decreased and your quality and uniformity greatly enhanced. An invoice is an invoice, for example, and there's no need to reinvent the wheel every time you want to get paid. In some cases, I've provided an actual template to apply rather than a checklist to follow, as appropriate to the subject.

INVOICES

Invoices are sometimes called statements, and it's a good idea to put both words on them, since accounts payable departments look for one term or the other. These should be sent promptly, and I advise sending them by courier to ensure they arrive and can be tracked. (Many consultants have waited months for payment of invoices that were lost. Proof of delivery is essential.)

Some clients prefer invoices to be sent electronically. That's fine, but make sure you use a template with your letterhead and logo imprinted electronically, as well.

By creating invoice stationery you can quickly whip these out by just changing the details. Note from the following template that they do not have to be extremely detailed. Expenses can be included on a separate form (see the next topic) with receipts attached.

On your computer, maintain a record on a spreadsheet of invoices sent, what date they were sent, when payments were due, and when actually received. This way, you can readily follow up.

On international billing, stress U.S. funds drawn on a U.S. bank. Include any payment schedules that apply, as well as discounts granted, purchase order numbers, federal ID numbers, and so on.

Invoice Template

March 3, 2006   No. 8101

INVOICE AND STATEMENT

For consulting work on employee sampling project, including scheduling, initial focus groups, survey design, discussions, and all related matters, per agreement:

Total Fee	$65,000.00
Paid on Commencement	$32,500.00
Now Due	$32,500.00

Total Due: $32,500.00
Terms: Due upon receipt

Thank you!

Chuck Jones
Creative Director
Acme Land Development Corp.
1007 Desert Rock
Rocket, CO 99999

Our federal ID is 22-000-0000 and our courier address is 85 Wisdom Court, Nantucket, MA 11111

EXPENSE REIMBURSEMENT

Expense reimbursement forms are useful for detailed expenses and long projects. Generally, clients (and the Internal Revenue Service) don't require receipts for amounts less than $25. Many clients demand original receipts (e.g., of airline tickets or hotel bills) and not photocopies. This is rather dumb, especially when you are trying to prorate expenses among two or more clients to save them money on a trip involving them all. (If someone insists on nothing but an original receipt, I then insist that they pay the full bill and it will not be prorated. That generally changes their tune.)

As with invoices, you should submit expenses promptly, at least once a month, and follow up assiduously if not received within 30 days.

Expense Reimbursement Template

A personal digital assistant is perfect for keeping track of expenses while traveling, including as many categories and clients as you like. You can then synchronize the resulting report with your main computer and either print out the standard forms included with the software or create your own spreadsheet, as I have done in Figure 6.1.

OVERDUE PAYMENTS

Overdue payments are a chronic problem in professional services, which is why I've always advocated being paid in advance, even if it means a small discount. There are times when payments are late because of client cash flow problems (primarily in smaller businesses), or because invoices are lost, or because mistakes are made.

But late payments are usually a product of either overly bureaucratic rules being enforced, or just sloth. In an age of computers, when a client says, "It takes 30 days to go through our billing cycle," it really means that your invoice is sitting on someone's desk for 29 days. And *every* client can override a system to generate a check tomorrow. Can

Consultant: Alan Weiss   **Month:** March 2006   **Client:** Acme, Inc.

Date	Air	Hotel	Taxis	Meals	Tips	Misc.	Totals
1							
2							
3							
4							
5							
6							
7							
8							
9							
10							
11							
12							
13							
14							
15							
16							
17							
18							
19							
20							
21							
22							
23							
24							
25							
26							
27							
28							
29							
30							
31							
Total							

FIGURE 6.1 Expense Reimbursement Template

you imagine a senior vice president waiting 30 days for a paycheck? I think not.

When a payment is in violation of your terms—say, 30 days—then go back to your buyer on the 31st day. (If your invoice is due "upon receipt," as are mine, allow a 30-day grace period for processing.)

The following letter is what you should send to your buyer. Don't argue with accounts payable or some processing clerk. Go back to your buyer.

> I need your help with something relating to our project agreement. Unfortunately, my second fee installment has not been paid, and it's now more than 30 days overdue.

(This can also apply to overdue expense reimbursements.) I've had occasion to use this gentle reminder many times, and rarely the last-resort letter shown in the template; but they're both important.

Some hints:

- ✔ Don't feel guilty or pushy. It's your money and they are violating the contract they signed or agreed to.
- ✔ Follow up weekly until your buyer has a satisfactory answer.
- ✔ If you're not paid in 60 days, use the second letter.
- ✔ No matter what excuses you're offered, remember that you can't use them to pay your mortgage or your kids' tuition.
- ✔ *If you're to be paid in installments, send an invoice for the installment 30 days ahead of time so that it can be produced on the due date.*

Overdue Payments Template

Would you please intervene with whoever is responsible in accounts payable to expedite this, and let me know what the status is? I know that you can probably do this in a few minutes, which is better than my making a dozen calls over the course of a few days.

Thanks in advance for your help. As you know, the project is going quite well, we're meeting all of our interim measures, and this is the only glitch to this point. I'll call you on Friday for our regular update, and perhaps you'll have some word by that time on this matter as well.

WRITING AN ARTICLE

I've encountered people who agonize over writing an article, yet know they must publish because it's such an important aspect of marketing. I'd like to simplify it, not by implying there is a formulaic approach that solely applies, but by suggesting that you can start with a certain regimen that will make you comfortable until you can adopt your own approach.

Any article, whether 500 words or 5,000 words, whether for a distinguished national publication or a local newsletter, has to be self-contained. That is, it provides a premise or point of view, specifics to be considered or followed, and a summary. The opening should provide a "hook" to lure the reader to continue. (Try reading the first paragraph of any article in the *Wall Street Journal*, and you'll soon find yourself on the last paragraph, so well is that publication written.)

The key is contemporary examples that make your points. There is no need for research, footnotes, or other academic detritus. Simply back up your opinions with specific evidence from the environment.

ARTICLE WRITING CHECKLIST

❑ Preparation:
  ❑ Understand the reader for whom you are writing.
  ❑ Understand the publication(s) for which you are writing (tone, style, etc.).
  ❑ Schedule time in your calendar (multiple sessions if needed).

❑ Gather research, examples, interviews, and so on, before writing.

❑ Writing the article:

    ❑ Begin with a working title and subtitle.

    ❑ Plan to establish 5 to 10 major points, depending on length.

    ❑ Create a sentence or two of introduction.

    ❑ Make each point and support each with examples, discussion, quotes, and the like.

    ❑ Create segue into next point, and continue process.

    ❑ Summarize at end with a paragraph or two of key points and actions.

❑ After writing:

    ❑ Ensure that your copyright, name, and all contact information appear.

    ❑ Spell-check and have someone else proofread.

    ❑ Rewrite only to the extent that more clarity is needed.

    ❑ Submit in hard copy or electronically, per publication specifications.

COMMENTARY

You should be able to write a five-page article in a single hour or in a two-hour session. Remember that these articles are seldom scientific or academic, and vast amounts of footnotes and research are not required. People are interested in your opinion supported by examples that prove your point in contemporary life and business.

You can submit the same article to multiple publications. Don't bother following up, because doing so won't help. Keep articles and article inquiries in circulation and you will eventually publish continually. When you write an article in response to an acceptance, be sure to adhere closely to the publication's specifications for format, length, and so on.

Template for an Article

1. Title ("Accelerating the Sales Process to Reduce Closing Time").
2. Subtitle ("How to Turn Every Salesperson into a Sprinter").
3. Compelling opening paragraph or two ("Ironically, there is no capital investment required to accelerate the sales process, yet most companies are actually spending money to slow it down. . . .).
4. The body: Compile 5 to 10 points, depending on length (1. Identify your all-stars. 2. Remove the bureaucracy. 3. Empower . . .).
5. Support each point with evidence, examples, diagrams, analogies, and the like (The Acme Company identified the top 10 percent of its sales force and asked, "What are they doing differently from the rest, and how can we further empower them while spreading the techniques to the remainder of the sales force?" The key differentiator was not product knowledge, but rather enthusiasm, *which these individuals brought with them at the time of hiring . . .*).
6. Conclusion and call to action (The seven points for accelerating sales are. . . . Tomorrow, you can begin by implementing the first two steps, which cost nothing and are quite painless. Invite your sales team to join in the process from the outset. Then . . .).

The keys are to be convincing, compelling, and conversational. Don't use footnotes or excessive references to other works. Use actual examples to which the reader can relate, so the reader begins to realize that he or she can use these ideas immediately.

Letter to Magazine Editor Template

I'm writing to suggest an article for *Today's Banker* entitled, "Selling at the Retail Level: You Don't Get If You Don't Ask." The previously unpublished piece would rely on my work with Citibank, Bank of America, and JPMorgan Chase at the branch level.

Specifically, your readers would learn:

- How to provide tellers with the tools to prompt new accounts.
- How to create need through questioning.

- How to direct customers to platform officers for the close.
- How to create and use point-of-transaction sales tools.

I've helped clients achieve 25 percent and higher new sales of products and services over prior years, *despite the economy*. There are testimonial letters enclosed from several customers—among your readers, I'm sure—who attest to these dramatic results.

As with many of your articles, there will be mini-interviews included, as well as illustrations of the materials cited. I can write the piece to your specifications and have it to you within 14 days of your approval.

My work has been published in *Management Weekly*, *Financial Matters*, and *Branch Banking News*, among two dozen other periodicals. I've appeared several times on CNN-FN to comment on sales in tough times, and I'm currently working on a book for Amacom called *How to Make the Sale the First Time, Every Time*.

I've enclosed an SASE, and have also forwarded this same letter by e-mail, in case it's easier for you to respond in that manner. Thanks in advance for your kind consideration.

SUBCONTRACTING

There will be occasions when subcontracting work to others makes sense economically and from a time perspective. The four main reasons for subcontracting are:

1. There is more work than you can handle alone.
2. The work required is uninteresting and you choose not to do it.
3. Special expertise is required that you do not possess.
4. Geography or conflicts preclude your personal involvement.

No matter how well you may know the subcontractor, it's important to have a written agreement covering your intellectual property, how the client will be contacted and by whom, expense reimbursement, fee levels, and so forth. You are better off with a few subcontractors you trust than a multitude whom you do not know well.

Subcontracting Contract Template

The provisions in this document will govern our relationship with Joan Larson while she conducts work on behalf of Summit Consulting Group, Inc., at the Acme Company.

1. You will identify yourself as a subcontractor for Summit Consulting Group, Inc. You will not hand out personal business cards or talk about your personal practice at any time.
2. You will do no promotion for your personal business at any time.
3. You will implement according to instructions provided by Summit Consulting Group, Inc., and will not agree to any altered, modified, or new conditions with the client. Any such client requests will be passed on to Alan Weiss for decision. You understand that all client property and work product will remain with the client, and all Summit Consulting Group property and work product will remain with Summit Consulting Group at the conclusion of the project, or prior to the conclusion if requested.
4. Your expenses will be reimbursed monthly, within 10 days of receipt. You will turn in expenses on the last day of the month. Reimbursement will include airfare at discounted coach rates, taxis, meals (not to exceed $75 per day), hotel room at the Marriott Downtown, and tips. All other expenses, including phone, recreation, and laundry, are not reimbursable.
5. Your payment rate will be $1,500 per day on-site and $750 per day off-site, as directed and approved by Summit Consulting Group, Inc. You agree that the work assigned to you will be completed within 60 days with a cap of 15 actual days on-site and a cap of four days off-site. You will complete the following work, even if it requires additional days but payment will cap at the levels noted:
   - Conduct 12 focus groups as assigned for 90 minutes each.
   - Analyze and produce reports on each group in progress.
   - Analyze and produce a report for the total group experience.
   - Meet with Alan Weiss at the conclusion to discuss the final report.

To download sample templates and checklists, go to www.summitconsulting.com. For more information, visit www.wiley.com/go/summitconsulting.

Fees will be paid within 10 days of the submission of your time reports at the conclusion of each month, provided that all individual focus group progress reports have been submitted.

6. All work created and all materials provided to you are the sole property of Summit Consulting Group, Inc. You may not cite this organization as your client in conversation or in writing, and all communications with Summit Consulting Group, Inc., and Acme are confidential and subject to the nondisclosure agreement you have signed.

7. You will conduct yourself professionally, observe business ethics and courtesy, and meet the work requirements above. Failure to do so in the opinion of Acme and/or Summit Consulting Group, Inc., will result in termination of this agreement and cessation of payment.

8. We reserve the right to terminate this agreement unilaterally with 24 hours' notice. If we do so, you will immediately turn in all client and Summit Consulting Group materials and work products. Upon such return we will provide the balance due you for outstanding fees and expenses.

9. Upon successful completion of the project, you will return to us within five working days all client materials, work products, and Summit Consulting Group materials, as directed.

10. You may not independently solicit this client for business for a period of one year following the completion of this project as determined by the date of your final expense reimbursement or debriefing report to us, whichever comes last.

Your notarized signature below indicates full agreement and compliance with these requirements:

_____   Notary, including signature, date, and seal:
Joan Larson

Date: _____   _____

FOLLOW-UP LETTERS

There are many occasions for follow-up letters, either in hard copy or electronic. These serve four purposes:

1. To keep in touch.
2. To establish next steps.
3. To thank someone for a courtesy.
4. To continue the momentum established earlier.

There is no need to reinvent the wheel and sit at the keyboard laboriously creating a new follow-up letter each time you need one. Following are templates for two of the most common: a new prospect and a failed attempt at communication.[1] (See Section 2 for a follow-up letter to a networking encounter.)

Note that it's always a good idea to try to enclose something of value, and also to give some options for future steps.

Follow-Up Template for New Prospects

I'm glad that John Martin introduced us at the fund-raiser Monday night. I'm sorry there wasn't more time to hear about your trip across the country!

Your work at the bank is very similar to what I've been doing with several banking, insurance, and diversified financial services firms, particularly in terms of cross-selling. I've enclosed "Ten Rules for Cross-Selling," which has been very popular among these institutions.

I'm in Hartford at least twice a month. When my next trips are scheduled I'll call or drop a line to see if we might get together for a few minutes or have lunch. I have some leads that might be appropriate for your people, but I'd like to discuss them in person with you before documenting them.

Good luck in the new position, and please give me a call if I can be of any help prior to my return to Hartford.

[1]My rule for people who don't respond is this: three phone calls and a letter. The three phone calls ensure that the original message wasn't lost, and the letter allows you to professionally close the loop without appearing either as a stalker or desperate.

Follow-Up Template for Failure to Make Contact

I'm sorry that we haven't been able to make contact again, because I had thought that our initial meeting was quite positive and that we had agreed on several concrete next steps.

In any case, I don't want to hound you. I'm here if you would like to re-open our discussions and would be pleased to try to be of help in the future. In the meantime, should other contacts within your organization develop further, I'll apprise you immediately of my progress.

All the best, and continued success.

Financial

Here we will deal with those financial matters that are critical to your firm's reporting requirements, growth, compliance, and so forth. These are internal (e.g., taxes) and not external (e.g., invoicing) needs.

TAXES

Your tax professionals are the best people to tell you exactly what is required, but by overview, consider the following:

- ✔ You want to avoid both business and personal penalty situations.
- ✔ You want to avoid a huge tax bite and a penalty by making periodic payments.
- ✔ You want to stay within the law in terms of deductions.
- ✔ You want to exploit and maximize legal provisions in your favor.

Depending on your locale, you will have state and/or local taxes in addition to federal assessments. Also, there is increasing pressure for reciprocity among states, meaning that you may reside in New York, but if you do business in California with a client, the California tax authorities want to assess the fees (which would be deducted from your New York obligations). In some cases, sales taxes are applicable, for example if you sell products on your web site or at speaking engagements.

In a C corporation, you should "zero out" the company earnings in the form of a bonus to yourself at year-end, avoiding the double taxation of business profits and personal income (which those business profits inevitably become).

Finally, in Subchapter S corporation and limited liability company (LLC) modes of incorporation, where business income flows through to your personal return, you need to make sure that formal paychecks are issued (and not merely distributions from the company to you) so that:

✔ You can satisfy IRS requirements for withholding.

✔ You can satisfy requirements for your particular retirement plan.

You want to avoid any red flags that may trigger an IRS audit, and you also want to be in a strong position should you be selected for a random audit.

TAXES CHECKLIST

❑ Ensure that periodic tax payments are made to avoid penalty situations.[1]

❑ Ensure that withholding amounts are appropriate; avoid penalty situations personally but maximize discretionary income.

❑ Leave no profits in the corporation at year-end (balloon payment in C corporation, distributions in S corporation and LLC).

---

[1]For example, if you fail to pay during a year either 90 percent of the current year's estimated tax or 110 percent of the prior year's, you will be in a penalty situation. These rules change, but they always include penalties and interest if you don't comply.

- ❑ Maximize income for retirement contribution purposes.[2]
- ❑ Check state and local laws on sales tax reporting, and acquire necessary forms.
- ❑ Charge your clients the taxes due as appropriate (e.g., tax on books purchased).
- ❑ Create annual file for all expenses and revenues by vendor and client.
- ❑ Set up a file area and maintain tax records for a minimum of five years.

COMMENTARY

One of the easiest ways to attend to tax matters is to hire a firm such as Paychex, Inc., or Automatic Data Processing, Inc. (ADP), to handle your payroll on an automated basis. They will report taxes electronically, and deduct appropriate amounts from your business account while making appropriate deposits to your personal account. The costs are very reasonable (e.g., depending on volume, perhaps $50 to $250 per month), and the results include forms containing all the tax information needed by your accountant.

Some people plan on a huge tax bite so they can have use of their money along the way, while some prefer to make estimated, regular payments. The key is to have a tax strategy created with a professional that maximizes your objectives while minimizing your risks.

INVESTMENT

I believe in the dictum that you "pay yourself first." Here's a good technique for investing money during the year (I'm not yet talking

---

[2]At this writing, you can contribute up to $40,000 to a simplified employee pension individual retirement account (SEP-IRA), for example, if that represents a quarter of your overall personal earnings, or $160,000. That is pretax money deducted from corporate profits, a wonderful opportunity for savings.

about retirement funding, which is somewhat different, and is covered next.)

Put aside 10 percent of everything you are paid by clients. If it's a $150,000 deal, put away $15,000; if it's a $2,500 deal, put away $250. Just pretend it was never paid to you and place it in a savings account or money market account. You'll find that it will grow dramatically, and 10 percent is about twice the average savings rate. Once or twice a year you can reallocate it to specific investments, or to a college fund or vacation fund.

If you invest corporate money (as opposed to money in your name), be very careful, since it needs to be relatively liquid (you can't leave profits in the company if you want to minimize taxes) and you don't want to take risks with corporate funds that may be needed later for operating expenses. (If you lose corporate funds in a bad investment, they are still on the books as taxable revenue.)

So, pay yourself first; be prudent with risk; and make the investments in your name, not the corporate name, unless you are buying property or tangible assets.

INVESTMENT CHECKLIST

- ❑ Establish a separate personal account solely for investments, with a bank or brokerage.
- ❑ Deposit 10 percent of corporate revenue checks once they have cleared your bank.
- ❑ Once or twice a year, reallocate those personal savings into investments:
  - ❑ Rainy-day funds for low cash flow periods.
  - ❑ Specific needs (e.g., vacation, schooling, medical, home, etc.).
  - ❑ Simple growth-oriented investments to maximize wealth.
- ❑ Check with a financial adviser as to risk, alternatives, legality, and so forth:
  - ❑ Pay a fee for advice—never seek advice from those selling investments.

❑ Determine proper allocation for you of conservatism versus risk.

❑ Coordinate with your general estate planning strategy.

❑ Monitor investments quarterly.

COMMENTARY

I've seen too many consultants who wind up cash poor because they have overinvested in their business and underinvested in themselves and their families. Remember that work is simply fuel for your life. No matter how high or low your business income, don't spend it all.

For those of you who are under 30, even if you are just starting out, make investment and retirement planning a high priority. Many older consultants are struggling because they thought that such issues were unimportant when they were younger (and their cash flow was healthier). Any amount saved when still young takes the place of much larger amounts required when you are older.

RETIREMENT

As a solo practitioner, retirement planning is strictly up to you, and it needs to begin yesterday. As a rule, you should establish a qualified benefit plan immediately upon forming the company, and make the maximum contribution you can to it every year. Period.

Your financial adviser can tell you what's best for your circumstances. In some cases, plans require that any employees also receive the same percentage contribution that you do, so if you intend to have people working for you full-time, that could be a major additional expense. That's why your particular circumstances are so important (and why I advise you not to have full-time employees if you can possibly avoid it).

Even non-tax-deductible contributions may make sense. At this writing, you can contribute varying amounts to an IRA every year (depending on your age) with after-tax money. Since the resultant appreciation of the investments is not taxable until withdrawal, when you may be in a much lower tax bracket, these after-tax investments can still make good financial sense. A SEP-IRA allows a maximum of about $40,000 at this writing (25 percent of paid compensation), but other qualified plans allow for even greater amounts if you are eligible and your financial people can arrange them.

Retirement planning is one of the most overlooked and ignored needs of consultants, often with horrible consequences. Set up your plan, maximize contributions to it, and monitor its progress.

RETIREMENT CHECKLIST

- ❑ Assess your retirement needs and assets given your current age.
- ❑ Determine your current assets and what growth is needed.
- ❑ Arrange for appropriate financial vehicles.
- ❑ Create a methodical contribution plan:
    - ❑ Periodic contributions during the year, budgeted, from company.
    - ❑ Use of zero-out bonus at year-end to make up balances.
    - ❑ Use of extensions in the event of poor cash flow.[3]
- ❑ Periodically, review best investment vehicles (e.g., traditional IRA vs. Roth IRA).

COMMENTARY

You can usually withdraw retirement funds without penalty for up to 60 days, so long as you reinvest them within that time. That can be useful for short-term cash flow needs or emergencies, but it is very

---

[3]In most cases, you can extend the prior year's contribution deadlines to well into the next calendar year with the proper filing, which allows you more time to generate the money, if needed. Of course, that puts you behind for the current year, but your cash flow may improve, allowing you to catch up and not miss a full year's contributions.

risky. If you don't redeposit them within the specified time and you have withdrawn the funds prior to the prescribed age, usually 59½, then there is a withdrawal penalty plus taxes assessed *at the original tax rate*. Thus, this is not a good idea for augmenting cash flow, even temporarily.

Seek out an excellent adviser who is not selling anything himself or herself (e.g., insurance, securities, etc.) to get objective advice. Remember to factor in spousal earnings, Social Security benefits, and other pensions and benefits that you might have accrued.

I'll say it one more time: Most consultants do not have adequate retirement plans for themselves at this time.

CREDIT LINES

These can be a savior for you. Primarily, you should have overdraft protection on each of your bank accounts of at least $5,000, so that you never bounce a check. (Deliberately using the overdraft loan for a month or two is far superior to dipping into savings or retirement funds.) If you have a personal banking relationship, overdraft protection accounts are easy to secure.

You can also arrange for credit lines in the form of a home equity loan, loan against business receivables and goodwill, or credit card lines. If you do create one of these, take out a loan quickly, and then pay it back within a month. That will immediately establish you as a good credit risk.

There is always the danger of dipping into lines of credit to create too much indebtedness but, if maintained wisely, they are lifesavers when the big client project is canceled or a check is lost or very late. They can also fund workshops, new products, and similar initiatives until they are able to generate their own revenue, at which time the credit can be repaid.

Some people believe in paying cash for everything, which is fine personally. But you can't run a business that way.

CREDIT LINE CHECKLIST

- ❏ Overdraft protection from bank:
    - ❏ Minimum of $5,000.
    - ❏ Automatically applied if account reaches zero.
    - ❏ Can be repaid at any time and should be on monthly basis.
- ❏ Home equity loan:
    - ❏ Provides checks to write to yourself or company.
    - ❏ Keep to a minimum to safeguard home equity.
- ❏ Company receivables and goodwill:
    - ❏ Bank must see your firm as a strong cash generator over time.
    - ❏ You are guarantor personally after company.
- ❏ Independent credit cards:
    - ❏ Grant in company name with you as officer.
    - ❏ Use personal credit card lines to loan company money.

COMMENTARY

All interest paid by the business on any kind of credit line is a deductible expense. That includes your taking out a home equity loan, paying the company the money as a loan, and receiving back the balance plus interest. You have a personal deduction (interest on the home equity line), a business deduction (interest paid back to you for the loan), and personal income (interest paid back to you for the loan). If you manage all that correctly, it can be highly advantageous.

It's important to document all loans between you and the company. Charge prevailing interest rates in either direction. Make sure there is a paper trail so that you can readily show the loans are legitimate and are being repaid.

A personal banking relationship can accelerate all of these plans and simplify the process, which is why I advocate giving a bank with such features the preponderance of your personal and business banking.

BOOKKEEPING

This is one of those business requirements that you're almost always better off outsourcing. Despite software on the subject, you'll waste a lot of time and make inevitable errors. Since this is an input to your taxes, it's highly important.

You can usually secure a bookkeeper for an hourly fee that may cost you anywhere from $100 to $300 per month, depending on the complexity of your return. Sometimes your tax professional can make a recommendation (it's too expensive to have them do your bookkeeping); sometimes your lawyer can recommend someone; and it's always a good idea to ask other local professionals whom they are using.

Make sure you get references and never commit to a contract. Ensure that the bookkeeper will create a computerized report in a consistent format each month. Some of these bookkeepers are freelancers who hold down day jobs or are stay-at-home parents. They needn't have an MBA or CPA degree, just an accounting background.

Provide the bookkeeper with your checkbook stubs, canceled checks, bank statements, deposit slips, and petty cash documentation (as well as credit card receipts if you take in fees in that manner). The bookkeeper should provide you with a general ledger, balance sheet, and itemization of income and expenses by category.

BOOKKEEPING CHECKLIST

❑ Systematic collection system: file or portfolio for deposits, check stubs, canceled checks, and so on for month.[4]

❑ Systematic exchange system:

  ❑ Notify bookkeeper when all records are available.

  ❑ You or the bookkeeper delivers and picks up (do not send by mail).

---

[4]Your personal receipts, for American Express, the local printer, and so on, should be kept in an alphabetized file for the year. There is no need to provide these monthly. They serve as long-term support and backup.

❏ Bookkeeper provides on computerized basis key needs:

  ❏ General ledger.

  ❏ Balance sheets.

  ❏ Itemized revenues and expenses by category.

  ❏ Net gain or loss for month.

  ❏ Comparison with same month last year, year-to-date last year.

  ❏ Additional copies for tax professionals as needed.

  ❏ End-of-year summaries.

  ❏ Hard copy and/or electronic copy, as required.

COMMENTARY

It's highly advisable to break down your income into categories, such as consulting, speaking, workshops, royalties, product sales, or teleconferences. That way, you can track what is making you the most money in terms of your investment of time and funding. You can code the deposit slips for the bookkeeper, so that if "1" is consulting revenue and you deposit a $10,000 check for consulting work, you write a "1" on the deposit slip copy that you provide.

Similarly, expenses should be categorized into travel, office, insurance, legal, design, materials, professional development, and so on, depending on your type of practice. That way you can easily see any deviations from last year or your projected budget for the current year.

PAYROLL

No matter what type of incorporation mode you have chosen (and ignore anyone who tells you that you don't need to be incorporated), you will need a payroll system. While you can do this with computer software or even manually (although some reporting is mandatory by electronic means in most instances), you are far better off with a payroll service that automatically takes care of salary, deductions, tax reporting, and the like.

The two biggest are ADP and Paychex. Both will deal with small and one-person firms. You need only have a tax ID and a separate business bank account. They can issue checks on an automatic basis, or you can call and specify each check, including withholding amounts.

Generally, these services can provide a check within 24 to 48 hours. They can electronically deduct the amount from your business account, send appropriate taxes to the respective authorities, and deposit the net into your personal account (or provide a manual check). You can see that trips to the bank and other "busy work" can be readily avoided, and these services, based on set fees and volume, can charge as little as $125 per month, which I think is a superb value.

They are excellent at complying with varying state and local laws, and also provide ancillary services, such as some types of insurance and compliance advice.

PAYROLL SERVICE CHECKLIST

❑ Flexibility:

❑ Maximum hours available, maximum days open.

❑ Ability to leave recorded voice mail message with information.

❑ Can provide regular, fixed amounts or individual checks.

❑ Maximum 48-hour transfers and applications of funds.

❑ Direct-dial numbers to a specialist.

❑ Can easily add people (e.g., should you make a spouse an employee).

❑ Reliability:

❑ Check references.

❑ Will reverse mistaken transactions immediately (yours or theirs).

❑ Compliance:

    ❑ Provides electronic reporting to all appropriate authorities.

    ❑ Generates required documentation for tax purposes (e.g., W-2s, etc.).

    ❑ Advises you proactively of changes in reporting and tax rules.

COMMENTARY

It's a great idea to have a consistent payroll specialist who understands your particular payroll needs. Extended hours can be important if you're traveling and want to call in a payroll from the road.

Overdraft protection, discussed earlier under "Credit Lines," is important for your checking accounts, since the company will always be paying *more* than the paycheck amounts (net pay) to account for its share of taxes, medical and life insurance benefits, and so on. You may sometimes forget this when looking at your available balance. (Be careful, though, because some banks will not use overdraft protection to pay a tax bill.) These services issue quarterly reports, which are useful to send to your tax professionals so that they can gauge progress and make any changes in withholding, deductions, and so forth.

Finally, it's very helpful to have a second signatory authority for your checks just in case you're not around and a manual check needs to be deposited (or someone needs to be paid). That should be your spouse or significant other, a family member, or someone else you can trust to perform that function when required.

Legal

T his section is intended to help sort out the legal needs of even the smallest business, from the protection of intellectual property to contracts and litigation. Any corporate entity needs legal protection in the marketplace, and this is a litigious society in any case. Never use the attorney who closed on your house or wrote your will as your business counselor, and *never, ever* use a relative.

INCORPORATION

You *must* incorporate. Occasionally, you will meet someone who advises you otherwise. I've even met two lawyers who insisted it wasn't necessary. Ignore that kind of advice (those lawyers also advocated dodging tax responsibilities). You must incorporate because:

✔ You protect yourself and personal assets with a legal firewall.

✔ You can create an entity with independent borrowing power and credit.

✔ You can create and protect certain benefit plans.

✔ You will appear as a going concern to clients and prospects.

The three common forms of incorporation are C corporation, Subchapter S corporation, and limited liability company (LLC). One may be better for your situation than the others, and only your financial adviser and/or attorney can best advise you in your particular circumstances. Traditionally, a C corporation form (which is what most major corporations use) allows for more deductions; Subchapter S and LLC forms allow for business funds to flow through to your personal account, making many transactions much easier; an S corporation has shareholders, while an LLC has members. The legal provisions frequently change, blurring the distinctions (I recently changed from C to S after 20 years, for example). Whether your spouse, significant other, or investors own part of your company, or whether you intend to employ people, will also affect the decision.

In most states and in most instances, incorporation is relatively inexpensive. It can range from a few hundred dollars to about a thousand. The annual fees are minor, and usually include annual report fees, filing fees, and so on, which amount to a couple of hundred dollars and an hour of an attorney's time on your behalf.

INCORPORATION CHECKLIST

❑ Select attorney:
   ❑ Specialist in the field.
   ❑ Solid references.
   ❑ Provides estimate of initial and ongoing costs.
   ❑ Takes time to understand your personal objectives and business.
❑ Select form:
   ❑ C corporation, S corporation, or LLC as your circumstances dictate.
   ❑ Consider beginning with one, changing to another if appropriate in the future.

To download sample templates and checklists, go to www.summitconsulting.com. For more information, visit www.wiley.com/go/summitconsulting.

❏ Implementation issues:

 ❏ Federal identification number and business name needed for bank account.

 ❏ Corporate seal often provided for use in signing contracts.

 ❏ Make name uniform on web site, stationery, listings, and the like.

 ❏ Will corporate name be your brand or not?

 ❏ Use federal ID on your invoices.

 ❏ Ensure consulting fees are paid to company name, not yours.

 ❏ You will not need 1099 forms from your clients for tax filing.

 ❏ Conform to requirements (e.g., annual meeting, annual reports, etc.).

COMMENTARY

Do not use an attorney who is not specifically skilled and specialized in small business incorporation. Usually, your tax adviser is a better source to recommend the actual form of incorporation, which you can then ask the lawyer to implement.

Don't worry so much about the name of the corporation, which needlessly delays many people. Your own name is fine (it never hurt McKinsey & Company or A. D. Little, for example). If you use a more common name (e.g., my legal entity is Summit Consulting Group, Inc.) you may want to consider a tagline on your materials if the name itself is not explanatory. For example:

Questar Associates
Helping organizations acquire top talent painlessly

Don't worry about your name being absolutely singular and unique. It is not illegal, for example, for several Summit Consulting Group, Inc.'s to exist (which they do). Names do not make or break business deals. But a failure to incorporate properly can break your business.

TRADEMARKS, SERVICE MARKS, REGISTRATION

These are legal options to protect your intellectual property. They are *not* the same as copyrights, which protect written expression and are discussed immediately following these options.

A trademark is the first step in the legal protection of a tangible, such as the name of a proprietary product (The No-Skill Saw™ or Talking Showers™), while a service mark is similar protection for a nontangible, such as a workshop or phrase (The Love Me or Leave Me Seminar^{SM}, or The Seven Percent Solution^{SM}). An attorney will do a search to make sure the name is not currently in use and there are no conflicts. If filing for protection is possible, the attorney will provide evidence of your ownership to the Commissioner of Patents in Washington, D.C. During that approval time, which can take six months to a year, you can use the TM and SM designations.

If the approval is ultimately granted, you may then use the registration mark, ®, to indicate full legal protection and ownership. (Hence, you often read or hear a statement like "Widgetwear is a registered trademark of the Acme Company."). Prior to that full registration, your protection attempt could be challenged or rejected by the Commissioner's office.

You cannot protect book titles, for example, or abstract concepts.[1] But you need a specialized attorney, because you'd be surprised at what you *can* protect. For example, a partner and I have successfully registered our workshop, The Odd Couple®, despite the play, movie, and television show of the same name, because our application is in a different medium (professional workshops).

TRADEMARK, SERVICE MARK, REGISTRATION CHECKLIST

- ❏ Select attorney:
  - ❏ Reference from incorporation attorney, tax adviser, or other consultants.
  - ❏ Obtain estimates of fees, timing, process.

[1]And in many parts of the world, even legal trademarks and registrations are hard to enforce. At this writing, China is the most egregious example of lax enforcement against outright theft of proprietary rights.

❑ Review your potential protectable property:

    ❑ Models, processes, methodologies, technologies.

    ❑ Workshops, seminars, speeches, presentations.

    ❑ Descriptive names, phrases, identifiers.

    ❑ Products: albums, CDs, manuals, performance aids, and so on.

❑ Use in developmental ideas: as new approaches are developed, consider names that can be protected.

❑ Implementation issues:

    ❑ Consistently use marks in *all* cases of usage, even correspondence.

    ❑ Reprint whatever is necessary to reflect the protection.

    ❑ Ask your attorney to take action on any observed intrusion.

COMMENTARY

There are web sites that offer trademark searches and filing for a few hundred dollars. In my experience, the searches are perfunctory and often result in filing for protection that is rejected months later. The monetary savings are relatively minor compared to the thorough and professional approach of an attorney skilled in this area. Don't try to economize on your intellectual property.

Remember that you must demonstrate use. When I moved to protect The 1% Solution: Tools for Change®, for example, I made sure that it was used consistently on cassette titles, newsletter titles, speech titles, and other products. You cannot simply protect an idea or cute phrase you have that has no attendant application.

Here is the language that appears at the top of every one of my newsletters:

> Balancing Act® is our registered trademark. You are encouraged to share the contents with others with appropriate attribution. Please use the ® whenever the phrase "Balancing Act" is used in connection with this newsletter or our workshops.

COPYRIGHT

A copyright protects the written word. I create a copyright quite simply, by indicating either of the following:

© Alan Weiss 2006.
Copyright Alan Weiss 2006.

You need either the © or the word "Copyright" (not both), with the current year. You may also include "All rights reserved."

While you can file formally with the government and you can send yourself a certified letter with the material, which you leave unopened as proof of the date of origin, it's not necessary. You can place the copyright on the bottom of the pages of your article or document, or once at the beginning, to indicate the words are your creation.

Within copyrighted text, you should provide clear attribution for anything that is not yours, with the author and the origin. You can copyright a one-page promotional piece or a 300-page book (you'll notice that this book has my copyright, not the publisher's, for example).

As a rule, copyright anything you write for hard copy or for electronic publication: web site pages, articles, columns, manuals, guidelines, sets of techniques, position papers, advertising, brochures, training materials. Someone may challenge a copyright by proving prior use, but, like a trademark, they must also demonstrate that they attempted to protect it.

Of course, ethically and legally, you cannot simply take others' writing, models, and depictions and use them as your own, even by trying to protect them. That is called plagiarism, and is punishable by law. And when you use others' ideas even *with* attribution, obtain written permission from them (publishers usually require it), and, commensurately, make sure that you grant written permission when you are allowing such use of your property.

COPYRIGHT CHECKLIST

❑ Discipline and coverage:
    ❑ Manuscripts, articles, columns, position papers, newsletters.
    ❑ Books, booklets, audiocassettes, product text.

- ❏ Web site pages, brochures, promotional sheets, advertising.
- ❏ Certain e-mails, advisories, counseling in writing.
- ❏ Reports, analyses, market assessments, surveys.
- ❏ Implementation:
  - ❏ Use function key to insert © symbol (on Macintosh created by "option G," for example).
  - ❏ Update your copyrights as you update materials (even minor changes).
  - ❏ Review copyright usage with your attorney once or twice a year.

COMMENTARY

Bear in mind that any kind of attempted protection—trademark, service mark, copyright—is dependent on origin. Whatever you create for a client while working for a client is generally deemed to be work product and, therefore, owned by the client (who paid for it). Whatever you bring to the client engagement that was originally yours remains your property.

That's why protection is so important for your intellectual property and writing: because you can prove *and physically indicate* that it belonged to you prior to the client engagement and is not work product. As a consultant, that is as much of a concern as is theft of your intellectual property.

You can include copyright protection on recorded works, such as CDs, audiotapes, and other media, by including the notice on the label of each device and on the cover of the packaging.

If you want to modernize an old copyright, simply make minor changes in the piece (e.g., a new example, updated references, another paragraph of explanation) and you can then signify © Your Name, 2000, 2006. For continually updated material (e.g., your web site pages) you can state © Your Name 2000–2006.

CONTRACTS

Some organizations will insist that you sign their contract even though you've submitted a proposal that could be signed and used for the same purpose. This is quite common with the government, some non-profits, and even some public companies. This means that the contract will be heavily skewed to protect the organization at your expense. You can rest assured that scores of lawyers have made the document as safe as possible for their client, no matter the lack of fairness to you.

In addition, such contracts are generic and are usually applied to vendors of computers and parking lot maintenance as well as consultants and coaches. So they tend to be inappropriate or irrelevant in may respects.

Don't blindly sign these in your anxiety to start working (and start getting paid). Frequently, the buyer can make alterations or agree with you separately that a provision won't be enforced. If the project is significant, it's worthwhile to pay your attorney an hour's fee to get a professional opinion on any hidden dangers.

This applies as well to equipment leases, rental space, storage space, web site design, and so forth. If someone offers you a contract to sign, it means they are trying to protect themselves, not you. Don't blindly sign it. You can always negotiate or go elsewhere if you must.

CONTRACTS CHECKLIST

- ❑ Overall strategy:
  - ❑ Never sign on the spot or simply sign and return unread.
  - ❑ Read carefully, and highlight questions for your buyer.[2]
  - ❑ If contract is highly confusing or vague, consult your attorney.

---

[2]Never argue with the lawyers or purchasing department. Always go back to your buyer, with whom you have a relationship and who wants this project to commence.

To download sample templates and checklists, go to www.summitconsulting.com. For more information, visit www.wiley.com/go/summitconsulting.

❑ Negotiating tactics:

   ❑ Ask for troublesome provisions to be eliminated.

   ❑ Ask buyer to agree informally not to adhere to certain provisions.

   ❑ Ask for more clarifying or narrowing language.

   ❑ Offer alternative wording or approaches.

   ❑ Indicate that your proposal and/or fees will have to change.

   ❑ If deposit fee has already been paid to you, begin work and simply do not sign.

❑ Key provisions to investigate:

   ❑ Changes in fee amounts.

   ❑ Changes in payment terms.

   ❑ Changes in expense reimbursement amounts or timing.

   ❑ Ownership of materials brought to client and produced thereafter.

   ❑ Cancellation advance notice and fees outstanding.

   ❑ Unilateral changes and alterations that client can invoke.

   ❑ "Scope creep" language, which enlarges project beyond your proposal.

COMMENTARY

The most threatening aspect of these boilerplate contracts is that they provide for unilateral, short-term cancellation of the project by the client (e.g., with 48 hours' notice) without any further payments to be made. They may also attempt to withhold final payments until after project completion and an assessment of results at that time. There may be a cap on expense reimbursement and/or an insistence on unreasonable travel (e.g., remaining through a Saturday evening for a cheaper airfare). Some contracts can also demand a return of fees if the client unilaterally determines that the project is unsuccessful (despite the metrics of success that you've specified being met).

Equipment leases and maintenance contracts can be heinous. Some automatically roll over unless you specifically send a certified letter canceling the lease. Others require that you purchase the equipment at the end of the lease. In general, with the exception of some computer equipment, long-term insurance and maintenance contracts are never worthwhile and are actually more lucrative for the providers than the actual equipment purchase.

If you have a good relationship with an intelligent attorney, you'll find you can fax these contracts to the attorney and receive a quick opinion with a minimum of cost.

Advanced Marketing

This section deals with the creation of "market gravity," a term I coined over a decade ago to represent your ability to lure buyers to you. When buyers approach you (as opposed to your seeking them out) the cost of acquisition is dramatically lowered, fees are no longer a significant issue, and your continual pipeline of prospects is assured. As a rule, the stronger the brand you develop, the more powerful your "gravity."

PUBLISHING ARTICLES AND COLUMNS

Publishing is a key technique to create word of mouth and buzz about you and your approaches. Your company's name, your name, your brand, and any other key phrases or trademarks can be prominently mentioned within the context of your appearing as an expert in your specialties.

Most people think of major media exposure in the *Wall Street Journal*, *Harvard Business Review*, *USA Today*, and the like, but these arenas are not necessarily the best in which to appear. A specialized publication, such as a magazine devoted to insurance executives or a newsletter that circulates among manufacturing operations managers, can be much more effective in reaching the particular buyers who can write a check for your value.

The mistake that most consultants make is that they write an article and submit it. That may seem rational, but it's not the most successful technique, which is rather to write a letter of inquiry first. Find the publication's editor's name on the masthead,[1] and write a one-page (hard copy or electronic) letter suggesting an article and listing a half-dozen bullet-point results that would benefit the publication's readers. If you send this by hard copy, enclose a self-addressed stamped envelope (SASE). Keep a half-dozen or more of these inquiries constantly circulating and you will receive your share of offers to submit. (A sample inquiry letter appears later in this section.)

PUBLISHING ARTICLES AND COLUMNS CHECKLIST

- ❏ Magazines and newsletters:
  - ❏ Read several issues to determine tone and length of articles.
  - ❏ Ensure from masthead that freelance articles are accepted.
  - ❏ Find editor-in-chief or managing editor's name.
  - ❏ Create inquiry letter, hard copy or electronic, single page:

    Brief description of article you suggest.

    Five or more specific points that will benefit readers.

    Brief description of your credentials and background.

    Thanks for consideration.

    SASE if hard copy inquiry.[2]

---

[1] Two excellent sources: *Writer's Digest* magazine, 9933 Alliance Road, Cincinnati, OH 45242, and its invaluable resource, *Writer's Market*: www.writersmarket .com/index_ns.asp. You can also consult the *Literary Market Place* (*LMP*) in your local library.

[2] Do not follow up. Editors receive hundreds of inquiries a week and will not respond to such calls. Simply keep submitting.

❏ Columns:

   ❏ Suggest a regular column to editors who have printed one or more articles.

   ❏ Send samples of three or four intended columns.

❏ Administration and delivery:

   ❏ Always observe deadline and length requirements assiduously.

   ❏ Place your copyright on all material.

   ❏ Refrain from using previously published material (identify it if you do).

   ❏ Provide clear attribution for anyone quoted or cited.

   ❏ Do not worry about pay—this is a marketing device (some pay, some don't).

   ❏ Investigate reprint rights, subsequent ownership, use on your web site, and so on.

COMMENTARY

The overwhelming preponderance of publications don't pay, although occasionally you'll receive a pleasant surprise. Most claim first North American serial rights, but some have more extensive demands. In return for no payment, negotiate your own right to reproduce the article, giving the publisher full credit. (Sometimes reprint firms have an arrangement with the publisher and will charge you as much as $1 per reprint for your own article, which is unconscionable.)

Negotiate to use your articles in your press kit and on your web site. You may make multiple submissions of the same story idea to many different publications, which is not unethical or unusual, but you can accept only one offer to publish it. No one wants to publish previously published material, although you may include excerpts of such material if you clearly identify it as originating elsewhere.

Ironically, some of the best places to publish articles are also the easiest to reach: newsletters and specialized, small-circulation

periodicals that target a select audience, such as small business owners, restaurant franchise operators, high-tech chief financial officers
(CFOs), and the like. These are also the easiest places to become a
columnist.

Finally, Internet publishing is an equally rich area. The procedures are the same. You can print these out in hard copy for reprints,
making sure to capture the logo and publication information of the
electronic source.

Inquiry Letter Template

Dear Ms. Lamont:

I'm writing to suggest an article for *Today's Banker* entitled, "Selling at
the Retail Level: You Don't Get If You Don't Ask." The previously unpublished piece would rely on my consulting work with Citibank, Bank of
America, and JP Morgan Chase at the branch level.

Specifically, your readers would learn:

- How to provide tellers with the tools to prompt new accounts.
- How to create need through questioning.
- How to "socialize toward a sale."
- How to determine a customer's unmet banking needs.
- How to direct customers to platform officers for the close.
- How to create and use point-of-transaction sales tools.

I've helped clients achieve 25 percent and higher new sales of products and services over prior years, *despite the economy*. Jerry Lubock,
senior vice president of brand operations at Bank of America, called me
"the single most effective sales resource in the brand banking operation
in 2005."

As with many of your articles, there will be mini-interviews included,
as well as illustrations of the materials cited. I can write the piece to your
specifications and have it to you within 14 days of your approval.

My work has been published in *Management Weekly, Financial Matters,* and *Branch Banking News*, among two dozen other periodicals. I've appeared several times on CNN-FN to comment on sales in tough times, and I'm currently working on a book for Amacom called *How to Make the Sale the First Time, Every Time.*

I've enclosed an SASE, and have also forwarded this same letter by e-mail, in case it's easier for you to respond in that manner. Thanks in advance for your kind consideration.

Template for an Article

1. Title (*Accelerating the Sales Process to Reduce Closing Time*).
2. Subtitle (*How to Turn Every Salesperson into a Sprinter*).
3. Compelling opening paragraph or two ("Ironically, there is no capital investment required to accelerate the sales process, yet most companies are actually spending money to slow it down. . . .").
4. The body: Compile 5 to 10 points depending on length ("1. Identify your all-stars. 2. Remove the bureaucracy. 3. Empower . . .").
5. Support each point with evidence, examples, diagrams, analogies, and the like ("The Acme Company identified the top 10 percent of its sales force and asked, 'What are they doing differently from the rest, and how can we further empower them while spreading the techniques to the remainder of the sales force?' The key differentiator was not product knowledge, but rather enthusiasm, *which these individuals brought with them at the time of hiring.* . . .").
6. Conclusion and call to action ("The seven points for accelerating sales are. . . . Tomorrow, you can begin by implementing the first two steps, which cost nothing and are quite painless. Invite your sales team to join in the process from the outset. Then . . .").

The keys are to be convincing, compelling, and conversational. Don't use footnotes or excessive references to other works. Use actual examples to which the reader can relate, so the reader begins to realize that he or she can use these ideas immediately.

PUBLISHING BOOKS

This is the "gold standard" for acquiring business (the "platinum standard" is referrals from one buyer to another, which is covered elsewhere in this section). You may never get rich publishing books, or you might get lucky and create a best seller (my *Million Dollar Consulting* has been in print for 14 years through three editions thus far). My worst-selling book was probably my book on strategy, *Making It Work*, which nonetheless accounted for about $2 million in strategy consulting work.

Are you getting the picture? Books are wonderful credibility statements and door openers, *if they are commercially published.*

Self-published books may salve your ego, and may be fine for Web sales or back-of-the-room sales when you speak publicly. But despite the occasional claim that someone sold 200,000 copies of their self-published book *Management by Watching My Dogs*, don't take it seriously. You must have a commercial publisher (e.g., John Wiley & Sons, Jossey-Bass/Pfeiffer, etc.) if potential buyers are going to take your expertise seriously.

There is a formula to creating a book proposal (never write the book first), which you can then send to an acquisitions editor or an agent. If you want to find an agent, ask authors who have successfully utilized one if they will introduce you and your work. You'll find additional resources for publishing and book proposals in the Appendix.

Book Publishing Checklist

❑ Proposal:
    ❑ Establish theme, title, and subtitle.
    ❑ Establish primary, secondary, and tertiary audiences.
    ❑ Create Table of Contents (10 to 15 chapters).
    ❑ Write introduction (one or two pages).
    ❑ Write one paragraph describing each chapter.
    ❑ Write one chapter in full (any chapter, about 20 to 30 pages).

- ❑ Write a competitive analysis of similar books.
- ❑ Describe uniqueness of your book (interviews, charts, tests, etc.).
- ❑ Describe your credentials for writing the book.
- ❑ Describe your marketing plans (sell on web site, during speeches, to clients).
- ❑ Submission:
  - ❑ Send to acquisitions editors by name (multiple submissions are fine) *or*
  - ❑ Send to agents by name, preferably introduced by third party.
- ❑ Writing the manuscript after acceptance:
  - ❑ Schedule in your calendar for brief, frequent periods.
  - ❑ Adhere to specifications provided by publisher for format and length.
  - ❑ Use as many clear, contemporary examples as possible.
  - ❑ Write with the readers' usage in mind.
  - ❑ Correctly attribute all material that is not yours; get permission to use others' works/quotes.
  - ❑ Make at least two backup copies.
  - ❑ Submit in both hard copy and electronic forms.

COMMENTARY

A hardcover book requires between 250 and 300 manuscript pages, double-spaced. First-time authors are usually better off with an agent. The standard 15 percent commission you'll pay on all advances and royalties is worth it in terms of the agent's advice, negotiating power, and contacts.

Be very patient throughout the entire process. A book generally is requested to be completed within about six months from signing a contract, and will usually appear in print about four to six months after submission. You will have to take on a great deal of the promotional effort. You can obtain discounted copies from the publisher (this will be negotiated in the contract) and you can also buy directly from wholesalers such as Ingram Book Group, which is often an even better deal.[3]

When your book eventually goes out of print, you can use "reversion of rights" to continue to publish it yourself if you so choose. Self-publishing is far more effective if you also commercially publish successfully.

Template for Book Preparation

Why Write a Book

- Second best credibility source (if commercially published).
- Establishes a brand with great effectiveness.
- Creates a downslope for continuous publishing.
- Forces you to connect and configure your own methodology.
- Outstanding source of passive income.
- Ego and fulfillment.
- Ongoing learning (understand what you don't know).

How to Write a Book

- First have something to say, or don't read on.
- Think of the reader and audience, not yourself.
- Don't just whine—offer solutions and hope.
- Focus on the pragmatic, not esoteric.
- Use memorable language, phrases, metaphors.
- Do not emulate others' success (e.g., don't write *Chicken Soup for the Turkeys*).

---

[3]Ingram will give you a 40 percent or better discount; if you pay within 10 days you receive an additional 2 percent discount; and you will also receive some royalties, since Ingram will buy the books from your publisher.

- Discipline, structure, and planning:
  - Create calendar time.
  - Create contingency time.
  - Ensure you are undisturbed and unmolested, but above all comfortable.
  - Use a framework (e.g., 10 chapters of 20 pages each with 5 points per chapter).
  - Use variants (mini-interviews, case studies, wackos).
- Don't write everything you know; *write what the reader needs to know.*
- Attribute meticulously, but don't borrow too much.
- Write conversationally.

How to Commercially Publish a Book

- Create a treatment:
  - Theme (title and purpose).
  - Table of Contents.
  - One chapter in entirety (any chapter, 20+ pages).
  - One paragraph about each other chapter.
  - Description of primary, secondary, tertiary audiences.
  - Half-page on your unique credentials.
  - Several pages on competitive marketing analysis.
  - Description of unique marketing assets you bring.
  - Distinctions of book (e.g., interviews, self-tests, etc.).
  - Estimated length and delivery time.
- Choose an agent or acquisition editors by name.
- Write cover letter and submit treatment; multiple submissions are fine.
- Don't jump at a contract; if you don't have an agent, use a good lawyer (not your cousin Louie).
- Understand that you will have to promote.
- Beware of advice from others.
- One book is an accident, two are a coincidence, three are a pattern.

Template for a Book Proposal
to an Acquisitions Editor or Agent

MILLION DOLLAR SPEAKING: HOW TO DRAMATICALLY BUILD AND GROW A SPEAKING BUSINESS

TABLE OF CONTENTS

INTRODUCTION

The full-length Introduction appears here following the chapter summaries.

The chapter titles will be punched up, but for now here are the literal descriptions. The intention is to cover all aspects on the route to a seven-figure practice, from topic development to marketing to mastery and celebrity.

CHAPTER 1: THE CURRENT AND FUTURE STATE OF THE ART

Professional speaking today is poised for a period of tremendous, but highly different, growth. It will no longer be centered on the rah-rah empty motivational talks that catapulted Tony Robbins to fame and that are now ridiculed on TV newsmagazines. The marketplace will demand expertise and pragmatism, and superb delivery will be implicitly expected. The old guard is disappearing, in any case. We'll focus on what the market really demands and what approaches will be most valuable over the years ahead.

CHAPTER 2: HOW TO CREATE OR IMPROVE ANY SPEECH ON ANY TOPIC

There is a basic formula for an effective speech, which can then be built into more sophisticated and varied presentations. But anyone can create a speech in a couple of days and smartly and readily ignore the rubrics of boot-camp-like preparation. For veterans, this will provide the shot in the arm to break into new areas. This chapter will include researching, validating, and formulating the content. In other words, this is the source to create a keynote that anyone can utilize.

CHAPTER 3: DELIVERY FOR MAXIMUM IMPACT

The platform performance isn't the artistic endeavor it's often cracked up to be. There are more speaking coaches than there are good speakers.

Therefore, superb delivery is easier than imagined if it's focused on audience behavior change and the buyer's objectives, and not choreography, memorization, and orchestration. Here we'll deal with actual stage mechanics, audience participation, maximizing impact, and so forth. The drama shouldn't be onstage, but rather what happens after you leave the stage.

CHAPTER 4: CREATING THE IRRESISTIBLE MARKETING PACKAGE

Speakers had better be strong marketers or they'll be talking to themselves. We'll focus on the specific contents of a press kit, with examples of each entry, including biographical sketch, client results, testimonials, position papers, and so on. There will be techniques for gaining testimonials even if you're new to the profession and for setting yourself apart from the crowd. We'll cover web sites, demo videos, sample audio, and collateral materials, as well. The question of whether a staff is needed versus using a virtual staff will be definitively answered.

CHAPTER 5: REACHING THE RIGHT BUYER THE FIRST TIME, EVERY TIME

The fundamental reason that the average professional speaker makes less than six figures, let alone reaches seven, is that he or she approaches the *wrong buyer*. The major trade associations and speakers bureaus perpetuate this error, because it's in their best interests to do so (commissions, advertising, and so on). We'll address how to reach the real economic buyer, when and how to work with bureaus and agencies, how to circumvent the people who simply want a fee quote and video, and how to avoid anyone who can't sign a check. This chapter and Chapter 6 will constitute strong buying appeal for the book in and of themselves. Sample speaking contracts will be included. We'll provide ways to control the bureau relationship and not be subservient to it.

CHAPTER 6: HOW TO SET FEES THAT WILL SET YOU APART

No one is worth very much for an hour onstage or a half day of training, per se. Yet speakers charge based on those time frames (largely because bureaus insist on it). We'll teach people how to set fees based on value, and therefore how to make more money from fewer bookings—rather than less money from more bookings, which is what most speakers resort to sooner or later. There is no sense incurring the risks in this business without reaping the rewards.

CHAPTER 7: BECOMING A CELEBRITY KEYNOTER IS EASIER THAN PIE

Contrary to popular mythology, it is easier to deliver an hour's keynote, be paid lucratively, serve the client well, and leave than it is to work like a dog for two days doing training, be paid poorly, and have the client complain that the training isn't working (because the client doesn't reinforce it). Celebrity doesn't mean *Oprah* (and, in fact, being on *Oprah* usually doesn't help, Dr. Phil notwithstanding). It does mean becoming exceptionally well known and talked about *within certain narrower-than-expected confines.*

CHAPTER 8: BRANDING THE BUSINESS

The secret to long-term success is in working less and making more. And the key to that is establishing a powerful brand (mine have included the "contrarian," "Ferrari," "Million Dollar Consultant," "Balancing Act," and ultimately my name). Branding doesn't occur magically or overnight, and the reader should begin the process immediately. We'll include more than a dozen high-powered branding techniques that will draw buyers to the speaker, leveraging on past success.

CHAPTER 9: EXPANDING THE ENTERPRISE

The most successful speakers I know today—those few, like me, earning seven figures—are also the most diversified, and that's no accident. We'll provide the practical routes to passive income, products, executive coaching, becoming a spokesperson, gaining royalties, teleconferences, retreats, consulting, and otherwise parlaying existing efforts into diverse avenues of income. One of the reasons that so many older speakers can still be seen regularly on the platform is not that they love the work or that they're in such demand, but that they can't afford to reduce their platform time. That should be a choice, not a necessity. We'll also cover follow-up business and repeat client business that takes one out of the realm of the one-trick pony.

CHAPTER 10: THE ETHICS AND RESPONSIBILITIES OF THE PLATFORM

The book wouldn't be complete without addressing what is rarely discussed these days: plagiarism, attribution, original versus secondary sources, client work product versus copyright, and so on. There is a great deal of dubious material used in speeches, including everything from urban myth cited as truth to generic stories claimed as one's own (and then retold by the next speaker on the agenda). For the first time anywhere, we'll deal with the ethics of the profession and how to stand out as an exemplar of professional conduct.

The Appendix will include sample letters, proposals, speech outline templates, follow-up letters, evaluation forms, and the like.

INTRODUCTION

The first time I ever spoke publicly, I fell off a chair and rolled under the table behind me. The first time I spoke as a professional, I received $750 for the entire day (and thought I had died and gone to heaven). During my speaking career I've fallen off a stage, seen a prior speaker use my exact material, endured three fire alarms and two medical emergencies, traveled 2.8 million air miles, and interacted with well over a million people in 54 countries and 49 states (I'm afraid to go to North Dakota).

I've also made well over $15 million. That's not as much as Tony Robbins or Dr. Phil, but it's enough to cover the mortgage with some left over.

Professional speaking constitutes a rewarding, value-laden, and lucrative career. It is singularly gratifying in the opportunity to interactively help others and adjust, in real time, to the audience and their reactions. It's a natural for people who are passionate, who have value to provide to others, and who have identified a relevant market need.

Yet the profession has not been kind to new entrants, nor has it enabled many veterans to build the kind of financial stability their contribution deserves. That's because speakers overwhelmingly undercharge and overdeliver, pursue the wrong buyers, and focus on stagecraft rather than client improvement.

Moreover, there are enough myths surrounding this business to bog down even the most determined talent. My intent in this book is to enable the veteran speaker to create wealth, and the new speaker to create a vibrant practice on the way to that wealth. We'll cut through the malarkey and find the meat: how to create value, deliver it consistently, be paid commensurately, and diversify so that the trajectory of your career enables you to work less and earn more.

Isn't that the way it's supposed to be?

I've mentored more than 400 people all over the world who are seeking to grow and improve their professional services practices. I've taken the best practices I've created, discerned, or borrowed (with permission!) to focus the reader on the fastest, safest, and most comfortable road to professional growth in the speaking business. And through the kindness of my friends in the business, I've also been able to include mini-interviews with some of the most successful platform speakers in the world *who are like you and me:* not sports stars or politicians, and not media gurus or celebrities, but highly admired and constantly sought individuals who have built, from the ground up, highly lucrative speaking practices.

If we can do it, so can you. And if you're already on your way to doing it, we can help you accelerate the process.

Within these pages you'll find the best contemporary advice on speech creation, marketing, repeat business, diversifying, fee setting, ethics, and every other aspect of modern professional speaking. The modest price of this book can make you a million.

Trust me, I know whereof I speak.

—Alan Weiss, PhD
Author, *Million Dollar Consulting*

THE AUDIENCE

The primary audience will be people in the professional speaking world. There are, by rough estimate, about 35,000 or more. The National Speakers Association (NSA) has no more than 10 percent as members, because many of the more successful speakers don't feel they gain from that affiliation, since so many neophytes are members. This audience also includes performers and novelty acts, such as hypnotists, ventriloquists, impersonators, and so on, who use these specialties to augment their appearances and delivery.

A secondary audience would be the vast number of people who seek to enter the profession (the NSA has an annual turnover of at least 25 percent of membership who can't get traction in the business). This population includes the tens of thousands who belong to Toastmasters International, for example. My book *Money Talks* (McGraw-Hill, 1997) has been very popular with new people, and has also been translated into Chinese. The international market is vast, and the book would not be written from a strictly American viewpoint.

Tertiary markets would include universities and professional trade groups (my books have appeared on the curricula of Wharton, Temple, Tufts, and Villanova, for example). Allied groups, such as the Institute of Management Consultants, Society of Human Resource Development, American Society for Training and Development, and American Management Association, would also be likely targets. I have spoken and/or written for every one of those groups, and dozens of others.

MY CONTRIBUTION TO MARKETING

I've now commercially published 24 books, which appear in seven languages. *Million Dollar Consulting* is in its third edition and has been a strong seller for over 10 years. I also produce more than two dozen other books, audiotapes, videotapes, CDs, and albums through my company. My web site alone has six-figure product sales annually, and my materials are on Amazon.com and other Web sources. *Million Dollar Consulting* is often quoted as the bible of the profession. *Million Dollar Speaking* should be positioned as the companion book.

I keynote about 50 times a year all over the world. In the past 60 days alone I've appeared in Santiago (Chile), Quito (Ecuador), Mexico City, Dallas, San Francisco, Los Angeles, Denver, Des Moines, Lakeland (Florida), Chicago, Boston, and Washington, D.C. In those audiences there were more than 3,000 people. In addition, I continue to work as a Fortune 500 consultant with major organizations around the globe.

My newsletter, *Balancing Act*, has a monthly subscription of 5,500 currently, and that number grows by about 5 percent per month. I have several highly qualified lists of previous product purchasers, who number over 6,000.

My mentoring program has included more than 350 people from around the world who pay $3,500 each to work with me.

Annually, for the past six years, a partner (Patricia Fripp, a highly successful keynoter) and I have put on our workshop, The Odd Couple®, in San Francisco. This workshop has become the most respected source of expertise about the speaking business in the country.

I estimate that my total exposure annually, from consulting, speaking, product sales, coaching, mentoring, publishing, newsletter, teleconferences, workshops, web site, and allied endeavors, is somewhere around 500,000 people.

COMPETITIVE MARKET

The only other books dedicated to professional speaking, as opposed to effective presentations for managers, such as Anne Miller's *Presentation Jazz* (Amacon, 1998), come from Dottie and Lilly Walters. *Speak and Grow Rich* (Prentice Hall, 1997) has wide name recognition. This year, however, I'm keynoting at the NSA convention and have attained far higher visibility.

Moreover, the Walterses are renowned for self-promotion. Dottie owns a speakers bureau and has a built-in conflict in her advice. *Speak and Grow Rich* is dated, doesn't focus on the business side of the enterprise (overfocusing, of course, on bureaus), and avoids ethical considerations. The market can readily support a strong book in the area of speech, practice management, and financial development from someone who has, literally, built a seven-figure practice from the ground up. Neither Dottie nor Lilly Walters has ever been a highly successful speaker herself.

Million Dollar Speaking will differ from the existing *Money Talks* in these respects, among others:

- It's five years later. This is post-9/11—a different economy, more varied global opportunities, shrunken retirement portfolios, a new emphasis on ethics, and so on.
- Mini-interviews with two dozen or more top keynote speakers.
- Separate, comprehensive discussion of ethics on and off the platform.

- Less on fundamentals (e.g., how to set up an office) and more on advanced tactics (e.g., how to quickly find buyers and avoid paying commissions).
- Clear appeal to the successful veteran as well as the newcomer.
- Condensed focus on creating a speech, and heavier emphasis on marketing the speech and making money.
- Up-to-date view of the Internet and electronic marketing, which is far different today.
- Five years ago I was a well-known, successful speaker. Today I am an icon, sought out to coach and mentor, and I pick and choose among my own keynote opportunities both here and abroad.
- Emphasis on diversity for speakers to broaden the practice and assure financial well-being despite the economy.
- Brand-new sources and listings.
- Templates and sample letters for everything from contracts to gaining referral business, and from invoices to securing testimonials.
- Emphasis on branding and market "gravity" to draw and attract clients.

OTHER CONSIDERATIONS

I'm prepared to:

- Include mini-interviews from my range of successful speaking colleagues, each one of whom has created a thriving business.
- Include specific examples and templates for immediate use.
- Include resources to choose bureaus, trade association targets, Internet promotion, and so on.
- Promote this book in the back of the room wherever I speak.
- Incorporate the book into my four-color, 12-page catalog, which is distributed constantly.
- Incorporate the book into my web site, which already does a thriving product business.
- Promote the book to the trade associations in which I have contacts and a following. (For example, the National Bureau of Certified Consultants recently cited me in its monthly newsletter as "the foremost

author on consulting and speaking in the country" and promoted several of my newest books.)

- If you think it's desirable, include a CD of one of my actual keynotes for people to hear and use as a model or an example.
- Promote the book in my newsletters and monthly product offering e-mails.
- Purchase a one-page ad for six issues in *Professional Speaker* magazine.
- Aggressively promote the book to reviewers as the companion book of *Million Dollar Consulting*.
- Consider a joint discount for the two books purchased together on Amazon.com.

Letter to a Literary Agent Template

I'm enclosing my proposal for a new book entitled *Retaining Customers for Your Life and Theirs*. The work is based on my 18 years in senior management in the retail business and the past four years consulting to that industry. During that time I've published 9 articles and 18 position papers on customer acquisition and retention.

The book's audience is primarily managers in any organization catering directly to the consumer, and it demonstrates how:

- Abandoning inferior customers is essential to retaining great customers.
- A problem is a sign of interest that can be turned into an even larger sale if salespeople know how to respond.
- Advertising wastes money when word of mouth isn't concurrently managed.
- If you're selling products, you're missing at least 20 percent of your potential profits if you're not also selling services.

As you'll see in the proposal, the book is invigorated by 20 case studies of current businesses and more than 30 interviews with major retail executives.

I've been told by Harry Jones that you're the best person to work with on such a project, so I'm looking forward to your response. If I don't hear from you before, I'll call at 9 a.m. your time on March 15. You are clearly my first choice for this material.

INTERVIEWS

Interviews in print or on the broadcast media are important methods to achieve visibility. Don't kid yourself: One interview will not make you a star, and I know dozens of people who have appeared on every show from *Oprah* to *Good Morning America* without so much as a single additional sale attributable to the appearances. (In fact, major media shows like those may be the worst places to appear in terms of the demographics of the audience.)

Don't be overly fastidious about the topics you'll comment on, so long as they are in your area of competency. For example, when I commented on the winner's tactics to manipulate his group on the original *Survivor* television reality show, a front-page feature article in the *New York Post* identified me as "one of the most highly regarded independent consultants in America," which went directly into my bio, press kit, and web site.

The best ways to garner interviews are to take listings with:

✔ PR LEADS, which provides tailored, daily inquiries from reporters seeking interviews and sound bites (www.prleads.com). Contact: Dan Janal.

✔ Yearbook.com, a passive listing that is provided for assignment editors, reporters, talk show producers, and so on (www.expertclick.com). Another outstanding feature is the ability to send free press releases every day to that audience. Contact: Mitch Davis.

✔ Radio-TV Interview Report (RTIR), Bradley Communications, 135 East Plumstead Ave., Lansdowne, PA 19050 (610-259-1070). You can place an advertisement for media interviewers in this twice-monthly publication, especially useful if you have a new book or some new twist for the talk shows (www.rtir.com).

The key to a successful interview strategy is to be interviewed *often*. You have to spend some money to attract people in the right places, but one sale pays for the investment for a lifetime.

INTERVIEW CHECKLIST

- ❑ Attracting interviews:
  - ❑ Place advertisements and take out listings.
  - ❑ Post past interviews on your web site.
  - ❑ Send out press releases about new ideas, findings, awards, and so on.
- ❑ Preparing for interviews:
  - ❑ Research the publication or broadcast source.
  - ❑ Try to find out about the reporter or show host.
  - ❑ Prepare written notes to review.[4]
  - ❑ Practice making *brief* responses (time is limited).
  - ❑ Develop examples and metaphors, which are very powerful on the air.
  - ❑ Rehearse your three or four sound bites to work in early.
  - ❑ Be at the phone or studio well before deadline; have backup number.
- ❑ Doing the interview:
  - ❑ Listen carefully to the precise question; repeat question if you need time to think.
  - ❑ Try to praise the interviewer without seeming obsequious ("Good point!").

---

[4]Virtually all radio interviews are done by phone, so you can actually refer to your notes. For television, review them immediately before you go on the air.

❑ If television, ask a professional for wardrobe, makeup assistance.

❑ If radio, ensure no background distractions (pets, kids, phones, etc.).

❑ Capitalizing on the interview:

    ❑ Obtain a tape for your use (streaming audio or video for your web site).

    ❑ Use a transcript in your press kit and on your web site.

    ❑ Splice together brief interviews into a longer tape.

    ❑ Make sure interviewer has all contact info (they tend to reuse good sources).

    ❑ Send out press release about interview, completing the cycle.

COMMENTARY

Beware: Never agree to "host a radio show" by paying the producers money or to appear on a cable television or syndicated show for a huge production fee (the latter most usually features a somewhat well-known name to attract an audience). These are little better than scams. They do not play to your audience in most cases, and everyone knows that you are paying to be the host or the guest. This is no better than paying to be in one of the ubiquitous who's who books that require only a check as their entry criterion, and everybody knows it.

Like the best politicians, make sure you have three or four sound bites that you want to insert in your responses, *regardless of what you are asked.* In other words, if the reporter asks, "What are the most important qualities in a corporate leader?" you respond with, "I'm asked that in my workshops on corporate accountability" or I researched the question in my book *Leaders on Leaders*, and found that . . ."

You have the greatest chance of being interviewed if you are provocative and will stimulate the audience, not if you are bland and echoing thousands of other so-called experts. Be bold in your statements and use contemporary examples to support your points.

Interview Response Template

Here is a template I use in response to reporter queries (e.g., from PR LEADS noted earlier). The power is in brevity, whetting the appetite, and strong credentials. Thus, there are a few crisp sound bites with the clear understanding that there are more, a powerful but brief personal description, and a short response that the interviewer can read quickly. I keep the last paragraph as a stock macro on my computer so that it is printed with one keystroke, and the first paragraph is created based on the story line.

Let's assume the inquiry is asking what the key forces are in modern teamwork. Here is my response. Note the sound bites incorporated and my complete contact information included, both for rapid contact and for accurate attribution.

Re: Your inquiry on teamwork

There are seven key characteristics of successful teams that I've discovered in my work for Fortune 500 organizations, no matter what the culture. For example:

1. True teams are not committees, where some people can win while others can lose.
2. The best teams are finite, and sunset themselves when the goal is reached. I call these "mission accomplished" teams.
3. Teams do not need formal leaders so much as they need rules of engagement, so that they can operate effectively in the chaos of today's corporate world.

I'm an organization development consultant with 24 books in seven languages and hundreds of media appearances, and I serve on many boards including the Harvard Center for Mental Health and the Media. Feel free to call.

> Alan Weiss, PhD
> President
> Summit Consulting Group, Inc.
> 800-766-7935 (401-884-2778)
> Alan@summitconsulting.com
> www.summitconsulting.com
> Box 1009
> East Greenwich, RI 02818

Radio Interview Request Template

I've published a dozen articles (enclosed, with my press kit) on attracting talented employees *without* raising compensation levels. Since your listeners include many small and medium-sized business owners all trying to hire competent people in a diminishing labor pool that is dominated by three huge employers, I thought that an interview with me would help them to:

- Stand out in a crowd of prospective employers.
- Learn how to attract talent using nonmonetary awards.
- Turn every manager and employee into a talent scout.
- Gain high-profile publicity for their business for free.
- Use community work to attract high-caliber people.

I'm the author of the soon-to-be-published book, *Hiring Top People in Any Economy Before the Competition Blinks.* I'll be happy to provide you with prepublication excerpts.

I can do a listener call-in segment, or a straight interview of any length. In addition, I'd be happy to make available my tip sheet entitled "Twelve Tactics to Attract Top Talent Tomorrow" for free (normally $25) to your listeners if they mention the show when requesting it.

You can reach me at the contact points on this letterhead. I'm looking forward to hearing from you.

PROFESSIONAL SPEAKING

This is a fabulous advanced marketing technique for four reasons:

1. You may be paid independently for speaking.
2. You generate visibility and recognition as an expert.
3. You may get press coverage for your publicity purposes.
4. The audience may be filled with potential buyers.

Not a bad way to spend a few hours, in my opinion.

You may be a keynote speaker (45 to 90 minutes) at a convention, or a workshop/concurrent session presenter (three to six hours). You should have a fee for a keynote, a half day, and a full day. You may decide to reduce or waive a fee depending on the attractiveness of points 1 to 4. (As a rule, I'll consider reduced fees or even pro bono work for charities and nonprofits, but *never* for a for-profit organization.

As a consultant, be sure that your remarks include examples of how you work with companies, results you've helped generate, advice you've provided, and so on. This kind of "soft promotion" will help buyers in the audience understand how they might use you and, most importantly, recognize that you are a consultant who happens to be speaking, not a speaker attempting to be perceived as a consultant.

Speakers bureaus and a variety of hard copy and online listings also help to promote you as a speaker. Your local chapter of Toastmasters can help you develop basic speaking skills, and the National Speakers Association (www.nationalspeakersassociation.com) offers international, national, and local chapter affiliations to build professional speaking and marketing skills.

PROFESSIONAL SPEAKING CHECKLIST

❑ Preparation:

     ❑ Choose topics consistent with your value proposition and expertise.

     ❑ Build a speech and/or workshop that conveys practical techniques.

     ❑ Use contemporary examples and your own experiences.

     ❑ Develop visuals and handouts to augment and promote yourself.

     ❑ Rehearse in safe environments (e.g., in chapter meetings, before friends).

     ❑ Utilize a professional coach if you're uncomfortable or unsure.

To download sample templates and checklists, go to www.summitconsulting.com. For more information, visit www.wiley.com/go/summitconsulting.

❑ Marketing:

    ❑ Include capability and descriptions on web site and in press kit.

    ❑ Create demonstration audio and video by taping the speech and editing.

    ❑ Provide demo/press kit to speakers bureaus and association directors.

    ❑ Inform your current contact list and clients of the capability.

❑ Delivery:

    ❑ Arrive early and stay late to network and develop contacts.

    ❑ Ensure a soft sell by referring to your work conversationally.

    ❑ Focus on the buyer's objectives, *not* audience evaluations.

❑ Postdelivery:

    ❑ Follow up with buyer and with all contacts made during the event.

    ❑ Tighten up and refine speech as needed.

    ❑ Add client to client list, seek repeat business, testimonials, referrals.

COMMENTARY

Speaking professionally is about pleasing the buyer who hired you and appealing to any potential buyers (or recommenders) in the audience. It is not about self-gratification and evaluation sheets. Speaking is a means to an end, not an end in and of itself, or a validation of you and your work. Too many speakers are confused about that, and consequently treat speaking as a personal quest for the limelight rather than as a business venture.

Ultimately, speaking and consulting should be a synergy, with consulting clients asking you to speak and speaking clients (or audiences) asking you to consult. But it's important to be perceived primarily as a consultant, which is far more credible and portends far higher fees than a speaker usually commands.

Here is a variety of templates to cover a gamut of situations in the speaking area and a variety of experiences among readers.

Speech Development Template

TITLE: ACCELERATING SALES THROUGH INCREASED FOCUS ON VALUE

OPENING:

- Should be about two to three minutes.
- Briefly state the objectives and intent of your talk.
- Use one of the following to gain immediate interest:
  - Personal story ("I was once the worst salesperson in Iowa. . . .").
  - Statistic ("The best salespeople make more than four times what the average salespeople make, but don't work four times as hard. . . .").
  - Humor ("The easiest sales are to other salespeople who swear they can't be influenced. . . .").
  - Relevance to the audience ("Every one of you is overdelivering and undercharging. . . .").

BODY:

- Create a list of key points, geared to the length of your talk.
- Support each point with statistics, personal experiences, contemporary examples, humor, graphics, and the like. Example:
  Point #1: The best salespeople question and then listen.
  - There are four basic listening techniques.
  - Henry Kissinger credits good diplomacy with listening.
  - Here's a graph showing the proportion of customer's language in a typical sales call.
  - My greatest sale came when I said only nine words.
- Use the above approach through your entire list of points. Assume each supported point will take three to five minutes, depending on your content.

To download sample templates and checklists, go to www.summitconsulting.com. For more information, visit www.wiley.com/go/summitconsulting.

- Take questions as you go or call for questions when the body is completed.

CLOSE:

- Summarize your points from the body.
- Restate the objectives and intent of your talk.
- Call for action—suggest what people can do immediately to accelerate sales.

Note: Never end on the question-and-answer segment. Always save your close for *after* you're through with questions.

Speech Evaluation Template

I've always maintained that the only feedback of importance after a paid presentation is that of the buyer. Yet many speakers seem to yearn for feedback from the audience, and there are people who can raise the level of their game by analyzing participant feedback, so long as they are not slaves to it.

Most feedback forms are worthless because they:

- Ask if the speaker was liked (sometimes you're there to provoke people, not to be liked.
- Confuse input (visual aids) with output (changed behavior).
- Mix temperature, food, lighting, and, oh yes, learning together.
- Are used immediately after the session, not later on the job.

In the evaluation:

- Don't use arbitrary numbers for rating. My "6" and your "6" might be completely different opinions.
- Use narrative and qualitative response, not just quantitative response.
- Keep it brief.
- Focus on the participant's potential use of the material.
- Never orient yourself to the feedback sheet in terms of creating your presentation. You are not there to achieve a high score, but rather to meet the buyer's objectives.

SPEECH EVALUATION FORM

1. How well did the session meet or exceed the stated objectives? Please check one box:
   - ❏ Exceeded objectives, in that I've learned more that I can immediately apply than the objectives promised.
   - ❏ Met objectives, in that all promises were met and I can apply what I've learned immediately.
   - ❏ Did not fully meet objectives, in that I did not learn all that the objectives promised and/or I did not gain the skills to immediately apply what I've learned.

2. To what extent was the speaker responsive to class needs? Please check one box:
   - ❏ Exceeded needs: Provided specific answers and examples, responded to all questions fully, and tested with the audience to ensure points were understood.
   - ❏ Met needs: Responded fully to all questions and used appropriate examples for our environment.
   - ❏ Did not meet needs: Could not answer some questions and/or did not use examples pertinent to our environment.

3. What three specific ideas or techniques do you consider most important for your job and/or career?

   1. _____

   2. _____

   3. _____

4. What change or improvement are you most likely to make on your job tomorrow as a result of this session?

   _____

5. If we were to present this session again, what one suggestion would you make to improve it still more, if possible?

   _____

6. What other suggestions, comments, or observations do you have about the program, its content, and its delivery?

   _____

   _____

Promoting Public Speaking Template

THE ULTIMATE CONSULTANT:

Going for the Close
What to Say After You Say Hello

A New Workshop Designed and Presented by Alan Weiss

October 17, 2006, Hilton Back Bay Hotel, Boston, Massachusetts

Going for the Close is an all-new program designed and delivered by Alan Weiss, PhD. It is a highly participative, interactive workshop that focuses on *the conversation required for sales acquisition* for consultants, professional speakers, facilitators, trainers, and virtually all entrepreneurs who own or manage personal services firms. (Alan has worked with every profession, from therapists and architects to designers and advertising people.)

    Benefits of the program include the following improved results and outcomes:

- Qualify buyers quickly so as not to waste time—find the right buyer at the right time.
- Use conversation, phrases, and wording that drive the sale forward and toward larger fees.
- Focus on value and turn around any discussion so that the topic is value (not fee).
- Relate your value proposition quickly and in a way that prohibits "deselection" by the buyer.
- Create powerful approaches so that you know what to say after you say hello.
- Take control of any meeting right from the outset.
- Involve the buyer in the diagnostic as to how best to hire and use you, your products, and your services.
- Become an instant peer and colleague of the buyer, and not a vendor, salesperson, or subordinate.
- Avoid being delegated downward.

- Avoid being intimidated by rank, surroundings, or volume.
- Be thoroughly prepared to respond to any objection, at any time, from any buyer.
- Swiftly (sometimes tactfully, sometimes not) move away from gate-keepers and blockers toward the real buyer.
- Never have to follow up once you've reached the buyer. (That's right, never follow up.)
- Create larger projects and longer-term relationships from the outset.

This unique approach, which focuses on the *words, questions, phrases, and listening devices utilized in the close*, involves extensive role-playing and testing. The program is 25 percent lecture, 60 percent interaction and role-playing, and 15 percent debriefing. In a safe but challenging environment, you will master the conversational techniques, skills, and questions that *will be immediately useful in your marketing and sales efforts.*

- Precourse preparation materials ensure that you work on your toughest calls, thorniest objections, and highest-potential prospects.
- The program job aid manual includes lists of questions, reinforcement of the learning, special techniques for unique circumstances, and a personal action plan. (Alan is notorious for not providing handouts, and this is the first time this unique set of learning materials has been offered anywhere.)
- During the workshop you can sit in the "hot seat" and either practice your own responses or try your toughest objections on Alan and learn his responses.
- You will have the opportunity to practice intimately with small learning teams within the larger group.
- You will have the opportunity to observe the "hot seat" and learn from a safe distance.
- The workshop includes a *30-day period of e-mail questions to Alan's personal e-mail address*, to be answered within 24 hours. Use this to practice before a sales call or to debrief after one, or simply to continue to hone your skills.

Major components of the day will include:

1. Finding the buyer and never letting go: corporate, midmarket, non-profit, or family-owned.
2. Outcome-based value propositions: creating an irresistible allure.
3. What to say after you say hello: how to be a partner and a peer.
4. There is no objection we haven't heard: responding through verbal martial arts.
5. The series of small "yeses": understanding your business model and remaining faithful to it.
6. The choice of options: how to collaborate with the buyer on the buying decision.

Alan Weiss is the author of more than 20 books published in seven languages. He has consulted not only with the corporate giants, such as Merck, Hewlett-Packard, Mercedes-Benz, and the Federal Reserve, but also with midsize to large consulting firms all over the world. His solo practitioner Private Roster Mentor Program has had over 250 participants since 1996. He is a featured keynoter on the lecture circuit, and his friends call him "the rock star of consulting."

Success magazine, in an editorial devoted to his work, has cited him as "a worldwide expert in executive education," and the New York Post has hailed him as "one of the most highly regarded independent consultants in America." His work has taken him to 54 countries and 49 states. He rarely offers public workshops, and this one is the only one scheduled in this year.

Register early to take advantage of savings. (Note: Past and present members of the Mentor Program may take a 50 percent discount from all prices.)

Registration includes the workshop, presession materials, workshop manual, refreshments, and postsession e-mail support for 30 days.

Prior to August 1:	$495
August 1 to September 30:	$595
October 1 to 17:	$695

Multiple participants from one organization may take a 15 percent discount on each registration. Payment may be made by check (payable to Summit Consulting Group, Inc.) or credit card (American Express, Master Card, Visa). Remit to: GoingfortheClose@summitconsulting.com, by fax to 401-884-5068, or by mail to Summit Consulting Group, Inc., Box 1009, East Greenwich, RI 02818. Cancellation Policy: Full refunds 31 days or more in advance of the session; 50 percent refunds or 100 percent credit toward future session 15 to 30 days in advance of the session; 100 percent credit toward a future session within 15 days of the session. *Hotel reservations should be made independently.* Our confirming letter will include local hotels in addition to the site hotel.

LOGISTICS

The program is being held at the Hilton Back Bay Hotel in Boston (617-236-1100). October is a fabulous time in Boston, from the Freedom Trail to the fall foliage. There are a dozen hotels at a variety of prices within walking distance of the meeting site. We will provide these alternatives upon registration, *but we urge you to make room reservations early.*

Registration and a continental breakfast begin at 8:00 a.m. and the program starts promptly at 9:00. There will be midmorning and midafternoon breaks. Lunch is on your own, from approximately 12:00 to 1:15. We will adjourn between 4:30 and 5:00.

ENROLLMENT

Please complete separately for each participant and e-mail, fax, or mail:

Date: _____

Name: _____

Title: _____

Organization: _____

Street Address: _____

City, State, Zip: _____

Phone: _____

E-Mail Address: _____

Amount Remitted: $ _____

Method of Payment:

    ❏ Check enclosed
    ❏ Credit Card:
    ❏ American Express   ❏ MasterCard   ❏ Visa
      Number: _____ Exp. date: _____
    ❏ I am a current or former member of the Mentor Program and am taking a 50 percent discount.

Upon registration you will receive an electronic confirmation as well as a preworkshop preparation document. *Thank you!*

Speakers Bureau Inquiry Letter Template

Note: This goes to the principal, by name.

    I'm writing you at the suggestion of Gloria Trevor, who recommends you highly.

    As you can see from the demo video and press kit enclosed, my specialty is global marketing. My audience is generally composed of senior executives who are responsible for sales, marketing, and product development. Generally, the three speeches I give are of this nature:

OUTREACHING THE COMPETITION: HOW TO FIND NEW MARKETS FASTER THAN ANYONE ELSE

Benefits:

- New market identification.
- Decision template on how to set product priorities.
- Minimization of launch costs.

OVERCOMING CROSS-CULTURAL MYTHOLOGY: HOW TO GAIN THE HIGHEST SPEED OF ENTRY

Benefits:
- Avoiding the seven cross-cultural myths that impede development.
- Making slight adjustments without major investment.
- Reducing translation costs.

FORGING GLOBAL PARTNERSHIPS: HOW TO MARKET WORLDWIDE WITHOUT EVER LEAVING HOME

Benefits:
- How to form alliances with far larger distribution entities.
- How to leverage someone else's local brand.
- How to gain huge profits through licensing.

I've included testimonial letters from organizations such as Pfizer, Visa, and Campbell Soup, as well as trade associations throughout North America.

My fee schedule is:

Keynote (up to 90 minutes):	$ 6,000
Half day (up to 3 hours):	$ 8,000
Full day (up to 6 hours):	$10,000

These are commissionable fees.

I'll call you at 10 a.m. on the 27th to explore whether we're the right match for each other. Thanks in advance for your consideration.

Letter to Trade Association Director Template

Note: This goes to trade association executive director by name.

I'm proposing that I speak at your conference on May 6 in San Diego with a presentation entitled, "How to Avoid a Strategy That Sits on the Shelf: Why Planning Is Killing Strategy." This is designed to fit well with the conference theme of "Searching the Future."

Among other advantages, the participants would benefit from:

- Specific tools to create a strategy of inclusion.
- Alignment of all individual objectives behind corporate goals.
- Separation of strategy (top-down) and planning (bottom-up).
- Acquisition of a template to apply immediately.
- Clear methods to use strategy as a real-time management tool.
- Real-world case studies to provide practice and discussion.

I'm the author of 17 articles and position papers on strategy and strategic initiatives, several of which are in the enclosed press kit. My work has included strategy retreats with Acme Corp., Bravo Institute, and Charlie, Inc., all of which are about the same size as most of your member organizations. In addition, I've enclosed an audiotape of several radio interviews I've provided on the subject, as well as a video of my presentation to the Minnesota State Bankers Conference on "Strategy as a Leadership Leverage Point." You'll also find several testimonials related to this topic and to my overall presentation effectiveness in the package.

I'll call you on Friday, February 6, at 10 a.m. your time to discuss this further. If you would like to talk before then, use any of the contact points on this letterhead to reach me.

Thanks in advance for your consideration. I'm looking forward to our discussion.

Letter to Visitors or
Convention Bureau Template

OPTION 1

I'm a veteran of the speaking circuit who happens to live within 40 minutes of the convention center and all of the main meeting venues here. I'd like to seek a relationship with you whereby:

- I can serve as an emergency reserve should a scheduled speaker be unable to appear due to illness or weather.

- I can be one of your priority recommendations for conferences seeking your advice on obtaining speakers.

My experience, testimonials, topics, and other related information are enclosed, as well as demonstration videotapes and audiotapes. Once you're viewed the material, I'd like to spend perhaps 20 minutes exploring these ideas and determining how we may best help each other.

In my travels, I'm often asked for suggestions about meeting sites, and would be happy to put your best interests forward whenever appropriate.

I'll call Friday at 10 a.m. to determine when we might meet. If you won't be in at that time, feel free to either contact me before then or have your assistant arrange something that meets both of our schedule demands.

Looking forward to meeting you.

OPTION 2

I'm writing to offer my services in two areas: as a speaker for those groups that inquire with you for resources, and as an emergency replacement when a scheduled speaker becomes unavailable at the last minute.

My work typically includes about 30 keynotes and 15 workshops annually for organizations, which have included Acme, IBM, Mercedes-Benz, Metropolitan Life, and McDonald's. My most requested topics are:

- Strategy: How to see what the competition can't.
- Teamwork: Turning bad committees into great teams.
- Leadership: Making every employee an owner.
- Conflict: How to create win-win-win outcomes.

I've enclosed my press kit and testimonial booklet, as well as a CD and videotape. As you can see, my office and home are only about 40 minutes from the convention center.

I'll call you Wednesday at 1 p.m. to explore a relationship and to see if you need more information. I've spoken at the convention center many times but never had the opportunity to meet you, so I'm hoping you'll have time for a brief meeting or lunch.

Speaking Contract Template

This represents an agreement between the Acme Company and Summit Consulting Group, Inc., as represented by Alan Weiss. Alan Weiss will conduct a half-day workshop for Acme at a site of its choosing on March 10, 2006, from approximately 8:30 a.m. to noon.

The session title is "Million Dollar Selling: How to Increase the Size of Any Sale at Any Time." The audience will comprise about 40 senior salespeople and sales managers. Alan Weiss will provide the proprietary intellectual property, audiovisual aids, handouts, and facilitation. Acme will provide the site, administrative support, scheduling, refreshments, and equipment (overhead projector and screen, two easels with pads and markers, a wireless lapel microphone). John Davis, vice president of sales, will introduce the session that morning.

There are three options available to Acme for this session:

1. Alan Weiss will conduct the session described, and create relevant examples and exercises based on our discussions prior to it.
2. We will interview five sales managers and five salespeople, read current proposals, and talk to three customers to use this information to create case studies and "live" application.
3. We will interview as above, send an electronic survey to all participants, talk to customers as above, and talk to three prospects who did not buy your services to create a comprehensive group analysis of current practices and enable the group to immediately build our sales techniques into current prospecting activities on a real-time basis. *Note that this approach would require a full day's workshop.*

The fee for option 1 is $9,500, for option 2 is $11,500, and for option 3 is $14,500. A 50 percent deposit is required to hold the date and for us to begin designing the day. The balance is due at the presentation itself. Alternatively, you may avail yourself of a 10 percent discount by paying the full fee in advance. Expenses will be charged as actually accrued and will be due upon presentation of our invoice subsequent to the session.

Please indicate which option you'd prefer, sign this agreement below, and enclose the appropriate payment.

Thank you for the opportunity to work with you on this important development project. Please feel free to call at any time to further customize the approaches.

For Summit Consulting Group, Inc.:   For Acme Company:

Alan Weiss, President   Title: _____

September 26, 2006   Date: _____

Advance Speaking Requirements Template

Client Organization: _____

Event Name: _____

Event Site/Location: _____

Client Contact: _____

Site Contact (if different): _____

Number of People Attending: _____

Group Description:

- Job titles: _____

- Average tenure in current job: _____

- Average ages: _____

- Percentage male/female: _____

- Greatest challenges: _____

Duration of Session: _____

Start/Stop/Break Times: _____

Special Needs Individuals: _____

Opening/Introduction Person: _____

What Precedes and Follows This Session: _____

Audiovisual Requirements:

- ❏ Overhead slides   ❏ 35mm slides   ❏ PowerPoint slides
- ❏ Video   ❏ Flip charts/easels   ❏ Whiteboard/chalkboard
- ❏ Lavaliere mike   ❏ Hand mike   ❏ Podium mike   ❏ Laser pointer

Mode of Dress: _____

Presession Work for Distribution: _____

Will Evaluation Be Used at Conclusion? (please provide copy):_____

Note: Please provide exact directions to location and provide a room the evening before with guaranteed arrival charged to the master bill.

Speaking Requirements Sheet Template

I'm very happy to be presenting at your event on [date] at [location]. I've indicated my audiovisual and logistics needs below. Please confirm that the checked items will be present, or let me know if something can't be provided. (If an item isn't checked, then that item isn't required.)

Thanks in advance for your support and assistance.

- Microphone:
  - ❏ Wireless lapel   ❏ Hardwired lapel   ❏ Hand mike
  - ❏ Fixed stage mike   ❏ Fixed lectern mike   ❏ Headset
  - ❏ Audience mikes for questions: ❏ standing ❏ handheld
- Visual Aids:
  - ❏ Overhead projector   ❏ 35mm slides   ❏ PowerPoint
  - ❏ Easel pads, markers   ❏ Video playback   ❏ Rear projection
- Platforms
  - ❏ Lectern   ❏ Podium on table   ❏ Table for notes
- Recording:
  - ❏ Digital audio   ❏ Standard VHS   ❏ Digital video
- Seating:
  - ❏ Rounds of __   ❏ Classroom: __ aisles ❏ Chevron
  - ❏ Theater: __ aisles   ❏ U-shape   ❏ Circle

- Introduction:
  - ❏ Enclosed
  - ❏ Will be sent
  - ❏ None required
- Breaks:
  - ❏ None
  - ❏ Of __ duration
  - ❏ Your discretion
- Product Sales:
  - ❏ Back of room
  - ❏ Your bookstore
  - ❏ In lobby or hall
  - ❏ From my catalog
  - ❏ Direct to my web site
  - ❏ Book signing
  - ❏ I will ship
  - ❏ You will obtain
  - ❏ Discount of __%
- Expenses:
  - ❏ Billed subsequently
  - ❏ Included in fee
  - ❏ You provide tickets
  - ❏ On your master bill
  - ❏ Air by ❏ first ❏ coach
  - ❏ Due at session

Please confirm with me at Alan@summitconsulting.com or Summit Consulting Group, Inc., Box 1009, East Greenwich, RI 02818.

Speech Introduction Template

Note to introducer: Please read verbatim!

Alan Weiss is one of those rare people who can say he is a consultant, speaker, and author and mean it. His consulting firm, Summit Consulting Group, Inc., has attracted clients such as Merck, Hewlett-Packard, GE, Mercedes-Benz, State Street Corporation, Times Mirror Group, the Federal Reserve, the *New York Times*, Avon, and over 400 other leading organizations.

His speaking typically includes 50 keynotes a year at major conferences. He holds the record for selling out the highest-priced workshop (on entrepreneurialism) in the 21-year history of New York City's Learning Annex. His PhD is in psychology and he is a member of the American Psychological Society, the American Counseling Association, and the Society for Personality and Social Psychology.

His prolific publishing includes more than 500 articles and 24 books, including his best seller, *Million Dollar Consulting* (from McGraw-Hill). His newest books are *Organizational Development* (John Wiley & Sons), and *Life Balance: How to Convert Professional Success into Personal Happiness*

(Jossey-Bass/Pfeiffer). His books have been on the curricula at Villanova, Temple University, and the Wharton School of Business, and have been translated into German, Italian, Arabic, Spanish, Russian, and Chinese.

He is interviewed and quoted frequently in the media, and is an active member of the American Federation of Television and Radio Artists. His career has taken him to 54 countries and 49 states. (He is afraid to go to North Dakota.) *Success* magazine has cited him in an editorial devoted to his work as "a worldwide expert in executive education." The *New York Post* calls him "one of the most highly regarded independent consultants in America." He serves on several boards, including the Harvard University Center for Mental Health and the Media.

He once appeared on the popular TV game show *Jeopardy*, where he lost badly in the first round to a dancing waiter from Iowa.

Ladies and gentlemen, please welcome Alan Weiss!

NEWSLETTERS

Electronic and hard copy newsletters are in abundance, and many people feel that the field is too crowded. But there's a reason for the crowded field (and it's the same reason that Burger King builds stores across the street from McDonald's—they know people are going there to buy hamburgers).

People like to read specific, brief newsletters that bring value to their particular interests and professions. And that's easier done than ever before.

Your newsletter should be a single screen on the computer, or a two-to-four-page (four-color) hard copy mailing. It should be nonpromotional, with your copyright and contact information prominently displayed. Provide as much value as you can, even from other sources (with attribution). If it's quick and easy to read, you have a much better chance of your audience taking the time to go through it and relating the value to you.

Monthly newsletters are probably best, with quarterly a distant second choice (too infrequent a contact). Promote the newsletter and archive back copies on your web site. Don't charge for it—this is advanced marketing, not a product. Cite it in your e-mail signature file, articles, position papers, and the like as a resource for people to consider.

Do not add names without permission to your mailing list, and always provide an "unsubscribe" option so that you stay within legal and ethical guidelines.

NEWSLETTER CHECKLIST

- ❑ Creation:
  - ❑ Target it at your prospective buyers and their concerns.
  - ❑ Create a simple electronic format, or four-color hard copy format.[5]
  - ❑ Create at least three issues in advance to avoid deadline pressure.
  - ❑ Consider using a Listserv for electronic distribution.[6]
  - ❑ Include as much of your proprietary ideas and information as possible.
  - ❑ Show your copyright and contact information.
- ❑ Administration and promotion:
  - ❑ Archive on your web site.
  - ❑ Include mention in your signature file, articles, and so on.
  - ❑ Seek reciprocal links and mentions with colleagues.
  - ❑ Consider listings, ads, and search engines.
  - ❑ Rigorously hit deadlines, maintain length, keep quality consistent.

---

[5]Use plain text, not HTML, electronically or you run the risk of symbols being scrambled and nonacceptance on some platforms. Hard copy, however, needs to be eye-catching and of high quality.

[6]For example, DataBack Systems at www.databack.com will automatically take subscriptions, verify, maintain the list, and allow you to mail at your discretion for very low fees. Always back up your list on your own computer, however.

❑ Consider letters and comments from readers for publication.

❑ Consider trademark protection if appropriate.

❑ Follow-up and assessment:

 ❑ Newsletter subscriber base should grow by a net of at least 10 percent per quarter.

 ❑ Validated leads and inquiries should be received from readers.

 ❑ Subscriber base should grow on net basis through word of mouth.

COMMENTARY

Always keep the reader in mind. You'll make far more headway by writing with their issues and challenges in mind, not your own. Keep on top of address changes and immediately remove anyone who complains about being on the list. On your web site have a formal privacy policy listed within your subscription information.

The only two tests of newsletter success are:

1. Are subscriptions growing in excess of cancellations?

2. Are we obtaining direct or indirect business from the publication?

Newsletter Format Template

1. Title (Example: *Teambuilding Accelerator*).
2. Explanation of newsletter purpose (one or two sentences) (Example: A free, monthly newsletter on teamwork, team management, and self-directed teams. Back issues are archived for free downloading at www.summitconsulting.com.).
3. Published by (your name or company) (Example: Published by Summit Consulting Group, Inc, Box 1009, East Greenwich, RI 02818; 401-884-2778; fax 401-884-5068; newsletter@summitconsulting.com).

4. Copyright notice and permission to excerpt with attribution (© 2004 Summit Consulting Group, Inc. All rights reserved. Permission granted to excerpt or reprint with attribution. ISSN 00-0000-000.).

5. Article of the month (Example: "The Future of Teamwork in Geographically Dispersed Companies").

6. Techniques of the month (Example: Ten ways to turn a committee into a team).

7. Promotional spot (Examples: Now on our web site, or Alan will be appearing at . . .).

8. Logistical information (Examples: How to unsubscribe, how to submit a letter, etc.).

Note: If you are publishing a hard copy newsletter, consider four pages with two articles by you, one page of techniques, and one page by a guest writer. Include all other information listed as well. Create a template so that the newsletter looks the same each issue.

Newsletter Subscription Offer Template

Note: In the examples, the newsletters are free. If you're charging, simply include your subscription rates and how you accept payment. At the end of the letter are options, depending on whether you are offering an electronic or a hard copy newsletter.

I've taken the liberty of sending you our newsletter, *High Velocity Selling*. I thought you would be interested in its contents, which focus on improving sales per professional, increasing the amount of average sale, and decreasing both closing time and cost of acquisition.

This is the only copy you'll receive unless you subscribe as indicated below. I know your time is valuable and we're all besieged with reading material. But I think you'll find *High Velocity Selling* to be a practical, monthly tool with which to immediately enhance your sales efforts.

Future issues will include:

- Should you hire content knowledge or sales skills?
- Behavioral interviewing tips to select self-motivated people.

- Improving telemarketing business by reducing call quotas.
- Profiles of five top salespeople in their fields.

To subscribe (electronically):

You can either respond to this e-mail with "Subscribe" in the subject line, or visit our web site, www.velocoraptor.com, and click on "Newsletter Subscriptions." All past newsletters are archived on that site.

To subscribe (hard copy):

Please use the enclosed reply card, complete the address information, and simply mail it. Or call us at 800-000-0000 and choose the "subscription" option, which will prompt you to leave the appropriate information.

FORECASTING

Forecasting attempts can be your undoing, since they are ineluctably overly optimistic, while sometimes a brief conversation in an elevator generates a $50,000 entry for later that quarter!

Nevertheless, it's often helpful to be able to look into the pipeline and understand what your future is looking like.

Some hints:

✔ Be conservative and pessimistic.

✔ Use objective criteria to determine what progress really is.

✔ Update the forecast at least weekly.

✔ The less in the pipeline, the more direct marketing you need to do.

✔ Even with business flowing, the pipeline should always be full!

✔ Put the forecast into a spreadsheet, and you can watch the impact on your revenues as you assess differing conditions.

✔ Keep it simple.

Forecasting can be dangerous from two aspects. First, we all tend to be overly optimistic, causing us to think that there is more legitimate work in the pipeline than there really is. Second, if our forecasting is overly conservative and we hit the numbers, we often pride ourselves on what is actually a subpar performance.

The following checklist and template attempt to walk a fine line between those two traps.

FORECASTING CHECKLIST

- ❑ Creation and preparation:
  - ❑ Simple form viewed daily electronically or in hard copy.
  - ❑ Easy to change and update.
- ❑ Content:
  - ❑ Arrange prospects so that dates of potential closure can be viewed.
  - ❑ Use percentages or ratings to *realistically* rank chances of closure.
  - ❑ Range should run from initial contact to proposal submitted.
- ❑ Usage:
  - ❑ Track to force progress in each account.
  - ❑ Use to force time investment in highest priorities.
  - ❑ Use to evaluate elapsed time and need to improve.
- ❑ Additional benefits:
  - ❑ Can be provided for bankers and lenders to show revenue potential.
  - ❑ Useful for comparison with prior year to gauge actual progress now.
  - ❑ Excellent tool to manage time and resources.

COMMENTARY

The forecasting system can provide solace for a solo practitioner to judge and validate actual progress. It can be used with investors, family members, or merely personally to understand one's realistic prospects.

You should view your forecasting template every day and make decisions about your time, follow-up, additional help, abandoning some prospects, improving your skills, and so on. It can be a core and fundamental aspect of your business model.

Forecasting Template

Prospect	Sales Sequence	Revenue	Projected Close	Probability
Acme Co.	3	$70,000	May	6
Questar	1	Unknown	Unknown	3
Drug World	5	$127,500	March	9
Lonestar	2	$15–35,000	December	3
Etc.				

Sales sequence:

1. Initial conversation
2. Buyer identified
3. Buyer met
4. Conceptual agreement achieved
5. Proposal submitted

Probability:

1–3: Low and hard to determine. Not a clear prospective client yet.
4–6: My value and their need are a match. Sale clearly is possible.
7–9: Conceptual agreement with buyer and proposal are definite.
10: Check has cleared the bank.

Qualifying System Template

It's important to be able to quickly qualify prospects and leads so that we can apply scarce resources and time to the highest-potential opportunities. Therefore, you need to create some qualifying criteria.

Following is a model I've developed (substitute your own criteria and ratings as appropriate). I've filled in the content to illustrate the usage. It's a great idea to run every prospective client through this quickly. (Just because you have only a few leads doesn't mean you should pursue them if they're not potentially valuable. You'd be better off spending the time on further marketing.)

Instructions:

1. List your ideal traits for a potential client.
2. Rate those traits based on 10 as of utmost importance and 0 as of no importance. You may have more than one 10 or any other number.
3. Fill in the actual traits that your prospect possesses.
4. Score your prospect's actual traits against each ideal, with a 10 being a perfect fit, and a 0 being a total mismatch.
5. Multiply the rating times the score in each category.
6. Add up the rated scores to get a total.
7. Compare the total against the ideal total (all 10s in scoring) and come up with a percentage of the ideal.
8. Decide which percentage minimum is required for follow-up and with what priority, and apply. I recommend nothing below 80 percent.

Note: If you don't have enough information to complete the form, then do some further homework. It will be worth it.

Ideal Traits	Rating	Actual	Score	R/S
History of using consultants	7	Use constantly	10	70
Within a day trip of my home	2	Overnight trip	0	0
Services or financial industries	6	Mortgage lending	10	60
Minimum of 250 employees	8	625 people	7	56
Financially strong/stable	9	#3 in industry	8	72
Buyer easily identifiable	10	VP operations	8	80

Total Rated Score:	**338**
Total Possible Score:	**420**
TRS %:	**80%**

In this example, given the ratings assigned to the ideal traits, the maximum R/S possible (all scores of 10 in every category) would be 420. The actual candidate scored 338, which is 80 percent, or a low "B."

REFERRALS

This is probably the most overlooked marketing potential in the consulting profession. We simply do not ask for referrals from our clients or others who are in a position to help us. (An insurance agent will invariably ask a new client for names of others who may be in similar situations, a primary source of new business in that profession.)

Seeking referral business should be done regularly, twice a year or more often, and it should not be perceived as asking for a favor. Every day you refer people to your dentist, lawyer, accountant, web site designer, and so on as a professional courtesy and gesture of goodwill, expecting nothing in return. But your dentist and designer probably have no real idea of what you do as a consultant, so even with the best of intentions they can't refer people to you (and there are people out there seeking help for their teams, small businesses, personal leadership, marketing, and so on, and mentioning those needs to their dentist!).

Here is an excellent opening gambit, which I give to you as a gift:

> "As you probably know, referral business is the coin of my realm, the primary route for me to obtain continuing customers (and, in fact, you and I were introduced by referral). Are there five or six people to whom you could refer me, knowing their needs and the kind of value I provide?"

It's as simple as that. If you ask enough, you'll get highly qualified leads who will meet with you. If you meet with enough of them, you will sell new business. If you sell new business, you'll have a renewing source of referrals.

Referrals Checklist

- ❑ Clients:
    - ❑ Current clients—buyers and important others.
    - ❑ Past clients—buyers and important others.
    - ❑ Pending or unsuccessful clients[7]—buyers and important others.
- ❑ Professional contacts:
    - ❑ Attorney, accountant, printer, designer, dentist, doctor, and others.
    - ❑ Trade association colleagues.
    - ❑ Past and present alliance partners, collaborators, subcontractors.
- ❑ Civic and social contacts:
    - ❑ Family and extended family.
    - ❑ Town boards and social contacts.
    - ❑ Athletics and recreation involvement (e.g., Little League, Girl Scouts).
    - ❑ Children's school affiliations (e.g., PTA, drama club, field trips).
    - ❑ Charities, nonprofits, pro bono work.
- ❑ Other:
    - ❑ Internet connections.
    - ❑ Political and fund-raising colleagues.
    - ❑ Hobbies and interest groups (teaching, hiking, stamp collecting, etc.).

---

[7]If you have reached the proposal stage only to be turned down, you nonetheless have a good relationship with a buyer (and others you've met). There is nothing wrong with asking for referrals, which may be readily granted to atone for the guilt of having rejected your proposal!

To download sample templates and checklists, go to www.summitconsulting.com. For more information, visit www.wiley.com/go/summitconsulting.

❑ Planning:
  ❑ Record in your calendar to methodically mine potential referrals list at intervals (e.g., quarterly).
  ❑ Send thank-you note for all referrals, whether worthwhile or not.
  ❑ Reciprocate, unasked, with referrals to your list.
  ❑ Track best sources and highest quality, and focus on those more frequently.

COMMENTARY

You mustn't be bashful about asking for leads and referrals. The best way to approach this is *not* as if you want to make a sale to someone new, but rather as if you want to provide value to someone your contact knows, as a win-win-win proposition. That's right—when referral business takes place, everyone wins.

Referrals are the "platinum standard" for new business development. A third party can hardly refuse a colleague's suggestion that you meet, so you've already overcome the credibility and "unknown" hurdles.

Even veteran, successful consultants fail to mine this sure vein of future business with regularity. You might as well stake out your claim.

Referrals Request Template

Dear Mike,

I'm writing to ask a small favor. As you can imagine, referrals are the coin of my realm in this profession. In view of our productive partnership and the results we've achieved, I wonder if you might provide some names for me?

Are there three to five colleagues, acquaintances, and/or friends, inside or outside your organization, to whom you can recommend me, knowing that they would benefit from the kind of value you've seen me deliver? I greatly appreciate any suggestions you may have, and I'd be willing to use your name or not use it as you see fit.

I'll call you on Friday at 10 a.m. to see if this is acceptable and, if so, who you've come up with. Thanks in advance for this courtesy. You know that I will readily reciprocate in every possible way.

REPEAT BUSINESS

I've long advocated that an ideal mix of business comprises 80 percent repeat and 20 percent new. My reasoning:

- ✔ It's very tough to bring in new business, but very easy to extend existing client business.
- ✔ Repeat business has virtually zero cost of acquisition associated with it.
- ✔ You need some fresh air and 20 percent new business each year provides it.
- ✔ You should be dropping the bottom 15 percent or so of your business every year or two in any case to make room for more profitable and challenging future work.

That 80 percent assumes that there are quite a few clients, and you are not dependent on just one or two to renew (a key mistake in this business is overreliance on a single source).

Counterintuitively, perhaps, the best time to solicit repeat business is *during the current project*, not after it. Again I'll remind you that if you perceive you are trying to make another sale, you probably won't be too successful. But if you perceive that you can provide additional value to the client in new ways and/or in new areas, then you'll probably be quite persuasive and well-received.

The first sale is always to yourself.

If you're not building a substantial potential for repeat business, your practice will inevitably fail, because no one can sustain growth based on acquiring new clients every single year.

REPEAT BUSINESS CHECKLIST

- ❏ Identifying potential repeat business during current project:
  - ❏ Observe and listen for areas of need, improvement, or repair.

❑ Mesh with your own core competencies.

❑ Prepare tentative approach and focus on value of the outcomes.

❑ Preparing buyer for discussion:

    ❑ Approach buyer when you are two-thirds done with current project.

    ❑ Mention issue on occasion and need for improvement.

    ❑ Provide free value as you both observe and discuss area in question.

    ❑ Get buyer involved in the value of the result of the improvement/initiative.

❑ Closing the business:

    ❑ Obtain conceptual agreement on objectives, measures, value.

    ❑ Submit proposal with options.

COMMENTARY

You will probably be the sole person considered for the new project. If the buyer decides to do it internally or to delay, you've still provided a great service and the opportunity to follow up later. Note how much more difficult this process would be if you waited until the completion of your current project and were not on-site frequently with ready access to the buyer for existing reasons.

Repeat Business Suggestion Template

Dear Joan:

I wanted to share some productivity gains we've seen in other clients with you because I know that you're always interested in these matters and because I'd be remiss in not providing you with this information in light of our prior and ongoing successful collaborations on succession planning and career development.

Virtually all of our clients believe that greater teamwork is essential to their efficiency and effectiveness, yet we've found that most of our clients actually have committees rather than teams. That is, their "teams" contain individuals who can win (reach incentive goals, for example) while others on the team lose (fail to reach goals). Senior management, like yourself, must continue to serve as referees and arbiters to settle disputes and create consensus.

I've been observing these identical phenomena as I've worked with your teams here on the succession planning goals.

In helping clients to sort through this, we've created a concept we call "aligned and self-directed teams"—groups that win or lose together, as a unit, fostering greater incentive to unilaterally share resources. In fact, we've noted these gains:

- Decreased turf warfare and boundary disputes.
- Improved resource allocation.
- Decreased duplicative and "failure" work to make up for others' poor first attempts.
- Decreased senior management intervention.
- Exceeded targets and quotas.
- Greater commitment and motivation to innovation.

I've enclosed some case studies and testimonials about the efficacy of this work. The next time we meet, which is in a week, I'd be happy to discuss how it might apply to Acme Company, given my knowledge of your operation and your philosophy about productivity improvement.

Looking forward to seeing you again on Friday, May 3, at 10:30.

PASSIVE INCOME

"Making money while you sleep" isn't merely a bromide; it's a very sound business decision. Nor is there anything immoral, unethical, or illegal about a consultant providing an array of products and services. In fact, those products can help to reinforce and spread your brand.

"Passive income" means to me that you derive revenue without having to visit a client. Hence, a teleconference you do from your home for an hour for which you charge listeners $50 (and which may be recorded and generate a CD product that sells for $50) is "passive."

The stronger your brand, the more likely that your products and services will be sought, and the more they are sought, the greater your brand visibility. It's never too early or too late to begin developing passive income. It's generally not a function of experience so much as providing value in the right context to the right audience.

For example, your clients may request booklets, newsletters, or CDs to augment what you've done for them, or the audience for those products may be individual purchasers totally divorced from your traditional consulting clients.

There is an array of passive income opportunities. I don't regard "passive" in this sense as "uninvolved," but rather as income derived from activities that do not require on-site client visits.

If you are selling products on your web site, make sure that you have a secure store for the protection of your customers, and a privacy policy clearly stated so that people can be assured you will not sell or release names and confidential information.

PASSIVE INCOME CHECKLIST

- ❑ Written materials (hard copy):
    - ❑ Self-published books.
    - ❑ Royalties on commercially published books.
    - ❑ Booklets.
    - ❑ Manuals, guidelines, checklists.
    - ❑ Newsletters.
    - ❑ Reports and projections.
    - ❑ Alternative distribution channels (e.g., Amazon.com, other web sites).
- ❑ Electronic:
    - ❑ Articles for download.
    - ❑ Newsletters.

- ❏ Specialized membership web site.
- ❏ Web-based seminars ("webinars").
- ❏ Audio:
  - ❏ CDs.
  - ❏ Tapes.
- ❏ Video:
  - ❏ DVDs.
  - ❏ Tapes.
- ❏ Telephone:
  - ❏ Coaching (performed by phone and e-mail).
  - ❏ Teleconferences.
- ❏ Combinations, such as albums of workbooks and CDs.

COMMENTARY

You can easily leverage what you do to create several income streams out of one. For example, a teleconference can be recorded to produce a separately sold CD. A succession of teleconference CDs can be grouped into a CD album with a specific theme. Print materials can accompany that album to reinforce the CDs with text, graphics, and workbooks. There are almost limitless permutations.

In general, print materials sell best, then audio, and finally video. What is termed "e-learning" and Web-based seminars have simply not caught on, nor have low-priced downloadable e-books.

You are better off with a few complex, high-value products at substantial prices (and, therefore, good margin) than you are with a multitude of cheap vehicles. Make sure that all books and booklets include both an ISBN number and a bar code, so that they can be sold by Amazon.com and other distribution channels if desired, and that they appear in sources such as *Books in Print*. Audio and video work can also be registered. (Newsletters receive an ISSN number.) These numbers, bar codes, and a wealth of other information can be found at the R. R. Bowker Company, www.bowker.com.

Teleconference Template

(*Note:* This outline does not represent an entire hourlong conference, only about a quarter-hour for me at my normal rate of speaking.)

TOPIC: HIGH PERFORMANCE COACHING

- Welcome:
  - How to access recording after the session.
  - Test mute button.
- What is coaching?
  - Working one-on-one to improve performance.
  - Relationship to teams and organizational performance.
  - Different from mentoring.
  - Subset of consulting.
- Vibrant field today:
  - Not new but more acceptable.
  - Credentials and certifications *not* needed, but methodology required.
  - Stops short of the therapeutic—must work within one's competencies.
- Possible relationships:
  - Hired and paid by individual client.
  - Hired by another, but confidential with person being coached.
  - Hired by another, results also reported to that buyer.
- Basic process (my bias, not "royal road") and strategy:
  - Meet with subject to discuss compatibility—discuss pros and cons, make mutual decisions.
  - Create proposal and accept assignment—never submit blind to human resources.
  - Establish rules of engagement—govern how both of you will act.
  - Launch and engage—ongoing fine-tuning.

(Another three pages would follow to complete the outline for an hour's teleconference.)

INTERNATIONAL BUSINESS

Even mom-and-pop operations are selling internationally these days because of the confluence of three major events in our business environment:

1. The advent of global competition, outsourcing, and truly global consumers.

2. High technology, which time-shifts orders and allows rapid communication.

3. Increasing respect for and embrace of diversity and new markets.

A consultant can certainly generate passive income internationally by selling a variety of Web-based products, for example. But a consultants can also work internationally more easily than ever before. This may be attractive for the additional source of revenue, the lure of exotic places, and/or the variety of new consulting challenges.

International business also looks better on your resume and can make the difference when you are competing for a prospect who has, or envisions, international operations.

INTERNATIONAL BUSINESS CHECKLIST

❑ Sources:

❑ Existing clients who have multinational operations.

❑ Foreign firms that have operations within the United States.

❑ Overseas management associations.

❑ Speaking at international events within the United States.

❑ Publishing in overseas sources, both hard copy and electronic.

❑ Local consulting firms working abroad looking for an additional U.S. partner.

❏ Preparation for travel:

  ❏ Read about the country, its culture, and its history.

  ❏ Check with your hosts about behavior and security.

  ❏ Insist on payment in American dollars drawn on a U.S. bank.

  ❏ Insist on a minimum of 50 percent paid in advance, and the balance when you arrive.[8]

  ❏ Adjust materials/approaches as needed.

  ❏ Make backup travel plans; secure any required visas.

  ❏ Consider renting an international cell phone.

  ❏ Explore other prospects you may visit while in the country.

  ❏ Check about customs and permits if you are shipping business materials.

❏ Delivery:

  ❏ Be sensitive to differences in starting times, breaks, feedback, and so on.

  ❏ Understand that electricity, water quality, phone access may vary.

  ❏ Your client is dealing with you in a second language—be patient and precise.

  ❏ Blend in as much as possible to local culture and mores.

  ❏ Take some additional time to enjoy the country and its offerings.

  ❏ Be prepared to socialize with client, sometimes extensively.

  ❏ Pursue local referrals.

❏ Postdelivery:

  ❏ Send a thank-you letter and/or gift (depending on culture).

---

[8]This includes expense reimbursement, and I'm not kidding about this. The transfer of funds can take time, and many cultures are much more undisciplined about making timely payments than we are. This is especially true if working for a new client.

❑ Include client, results, experience, and so on, on your web site and in press kit.

❑ Follow up immediately on any unpaid billing or obligations.

COMMENTARY

For better or for worse, American English has become the world's language, the dollar is the world's currency, and our culture has become the world's overarching influence. I make no value judgments, just state facts. When I spoke in Santiago, Chile, not long ago, my hosts spoke perfect English, I was lodged in a Sheraton Hotel, the cocktail waitress spoke English, I purchased a *Miami Herald* at the gift shop with American dollars, and the combo in the lounge was playing Cole Porter tunes.

I could have been in Florida.

Peter Drucker points out that one of the strongest continuing American exports is likely to be management expertise. My Australian friends gauge progress partially by how far behind the United States they are in trends and fashion.

Never accept local money in payment, nor checks that are not drawn on American banks, because the exchange fees can be very significant.

Allow yourself at least a full day to acclimate after long flights in any direction. Most long-distance flights are overnight. Try to learn enough of the local language to order meals, talk to hotel clerks, and give a cab driver directions. Your hosts will also appreciate that gesture.

ALLIANCES

Alliances are not loosely knit collaborations or the mere exchange of business cards with the nebulous promise, "Let's do something together." Alliances are great ways—particularly for newer consultants, but also for veterans—to exponentially grow the business.

An alliance partner should ideally have these characteristics:

✔ Is larger than you are in revenue, scope, size.

✔ Possesses strength you don't have (e.g., distribution).

✔ Needs your strength (e.g., coaching, classroom training).

✔ Puts money and/or business on the table, not a future possibility.

✔ Provides principal or owner as your contact.

Don't confuse an alliance with subcontracting. When you subcontract for someone, you are paid a set fee to perform in a manner dictated by the contractor, and you are usually not part of the value-added inducement. You are an implementer, often prohibited from any initiation with the client.

As an alliance partner, you help to establish what the fees are, what the expenses should be, how the profit is split, how you are identified, what you will and will not do, your independent role with the clients, and so forth. That's a true partnership.

Alliances in which 1 + 1 = 64 don't come along too often. (You'll be investing time, energy, and money in the alliance, so you need a substantially larger business as a result.)

ALLIANCE CHECKLIST

❑ Sources:

❑ Other consulting firms or individuals.

❑ Providers, suppliers, vendors.

❑ Conference facilities, production companies, producers.

❑ Audio/video professionals, publishers, newsletters, web sites.

❑ Other professional services (e.g., compliance, insurance, finance, etc.).

❑ Chemistry and trust:

- ❏ You are comfortable with them socially and conversationally.
- ❏ They share their financials, strategy, plans, and so on.
- ❏ You are comfortable sharing your financials, strategy, plans, and so on.
- ❏ Meet frequently over prolonged period to ensure comfort.
- ❏ Due diligence:
  - ❏ Visit and observe operation/work with clients.
  - ❏ Have your financial professionals review their financial statements.
  - ❏ Ask for and check client references.
  - ❏ Talk to present (and past, if possible) employees.
  - ❏ Meet all senior/key people.
  - ❏ There is immediate or short-term joint business on the table.
- ❏ Legal and formal issues:
  - ❏ Positioning of the names and brands involved.
  - ❏ Contribution to expenses, share of profits.
  - ❏ Representations to client, follow-up, repeat and spin-off business.
  - ❏ Unilateral right to terminate arrangements with proper notice.
  - ❏ Ownership of preexisting and jointly created intellectual property/materials.
  - ❏ Invoicing, tax reporting, terms between client and alliance partners.

COMMENTARY

A large publishing and research firm that had enormous distribution, lists, and marketing devices entered into an alliance with me to which I brought my intellectual property regarding consulting techniques, my brand, and my speaking abilities. As a result, we sponsored and ran "rainmaking" seminars for several years, the firm asked me to edit one of its newsletters, and it published three of my high-end books.

This is just one example of such an alliance partnership. Alliances are a marvelous mechanism for the solo practitioner to exponentially increase bandwidth, brand visibility, and bottom-line business.

RETAINERS

Retainers are monthly, quarterly, semiannual, or annual fee payments in return for access to your "smarts." They are not a retainer in the attorney's sense, wherein billable hours are deducted from a deposit. Nor are they lump-sum fees for project work, which should be based on the value of that project for the client (and which involve your active involvement and supervision).

A retainer represents a sounding-board arrangement for advice and counsel. You could have a retainer arrangement (and I have) in which you never, ever appear on-site. Your access is limited to—or is sufficiently provided by—phone, fax, and e-mail.

My belief is that a month is a minimal retainer period and that all retainer fees are due at the beginning of the period. For example, a $10,000 monthly retainer would be due on the first of that month, and a $25,000 quarterly retainer would be due on the first day of that quarter. This is for unlimited access, subject to your schedule and availability, and should usually be restricted to one or two executives. (Being on retainer to a team or committee can involve an inordinate amount of work if they all choose to contact you daily and/or if there is infighting among the members.)

Generally you can reduce your retainer as an incentive for a longer time period. For example:

✔ One month is $10,000.

✔ One quarter is $25,000.

✔ A half year is $40,000.

✔ A full year is $75,000.

Remember: All of these fees would be paid in advance. You do not guarantee a set number of days, only access to you. In my entire career, not one client has ever abused or tried to maximize contact in a retainer relationship.

Maximizing Success

I know that a "checklist for happiness" doesn't exist, but in this section we'll discuss how to ensure reasonable and fulfilling life balance, and how to analyze whether (and how) to sell your firm at some point when other interests beckon.

LIFE BALANCE

I've never believed that life balance was about achieving some perfect equilibrium between personal and professional time investment. You don't have a personal life and a professional life—you have a *life*, period.

Instead, I believe that balance connotes the flexibility to work and play when the spirit moves you, and to alter your focus without restraint or constraint. You may be writing a proposal on a Saturday morning and attending your kid's soccer game on Wednesday afternoon.

Work is merely fuel for our lives. No one regrets, at life's conclusion, not spending more time in the office, but many regret not spending more time with family. The beauty of the life of a sole practitioner is that he or she is beholden to no one. You can work as much or as little as you like, so long as you achieve the economic goals necessary for your chosen lifestyle. And that lifestyle is yours to choose.

At the beginning of your career, the launch and establishment of a new practice will demand, of necessity, more of your discretionary time. But as the trajectory of your career advances, you should assume more and more control over your time until you are deciding when and where to work. You can actually arrive rather early at a point where you can refuse to take on additional business (and even fire existing clients who are more trouble than they are worth—and we've all experienced them).

It's never too early to consider the life balance issues that are important to you, and it's never too late to improve imbalances that are causing stress and missed opportunities. The great thing about a solo practice is that there is no "they" to blame. *You are they!*

LIFE BALANCE CHECKLIST

- ❏ Time balance:
  - ❏ Avoid long "to do" lists, and get things done promptly.
  - ❏ Hit deadlines and fulfill the expectations of others.
  - ❏ Get a full night's sleep—minimum of seven hours.
  - ❏ Pay bills on time, complete reading material, file all reference needs.
  - ❏ Build in time for regular exercise—at least an hour every other day.
  - ❏ Spend daily time with family, friends, and significant others (even traveling).
  - ❏ Take at least one vacation of some sort every quarter.
  - ❏ Break projects into manageable pieces and schedule them in your calendar.
  - ❏ Ensure that emergencies and surprises can be accommodated without traumatic change.
  - ❏ Pursue recreation, hobbies, new interests, sports, and similar activities regularly.

To download sample templates and checklists, go to www.summitconsulting.com. For more information, visit www.wiley.com/go/summitconsulting.

❑ Fulfillment balance:

   ❑ You have loving relationships.

   ❑ You have a support infrastructure for advice, for help in times of trouble, and so on.

   ❑ Every year you achieve some of your aspirations and life goals.

   ❑ You have the freedom to fail, and to attempt and try out new endeavors.

   ❑ You are happy with your appearance, poise, and social initiating.

   ❑ You are sought after as an authority, board member, adviser, expert, and so forth.

   ❑ You are able to resolve conflict constructively and do not harbor grudges.

   ❑ You are stress-free most of the time.

   ❑ You like to laugh and often do so.

   ❑ You are relied upon by others and contribute your time, energy, and money.

COMMENTARY

Ask yourself if you are happier today than you were a year ago—more engaged, contributing more, achieving more personal and professional goals. Ultimately, your personal and professional lives should meld into a seamless approach to the world around you.

Everyone's life balance looks a bit different, because we have differing goals and interests, diverse backgrounds and circumstances. The sole determinant of successful life balance for yourself is you, which is why most of the gurus on television pitching books and tapes and "life experiences" can't help you, even if what they were peddling was more than vapid nonsense.

One of the finest ways to achieve contentment is to help others achieve it. We have no more right to consume happiness without creating it than we do to consume wealth without creating it. As you are able to manage your life so that you contribute to the environment around you, you'll find that you're achieving a life balance that is as natural and self-perpetuating as breathing.

REINVENTING YOURSELF

One of the worst things that can befall a consultant is that the consultant becomes better and better at what he or she is already good at, becoming an expert in an increasingly narrow endeavor. We've all seen the consultants (coaches, trainers, facilitators, speakers, etc.) who can do it blindfolded, and might as well be doing it that way for all the lack of innovation and creativity they bring to the table.

It's tough to advise a client on change if you're not changing yourself, and it's difficult to recommend creativity if you haven't been very creative yourself. The time to grow and stretch is from a position of strength, not desperation; so, ironically, the best time to seek change is when you're doing very well—hence this segment in the section on maximizing success.

Avoid the success trap by avoiding the plateau that success can create, as exemplified by the S-curve scenario shown in Figure 10.1. All practices will grow dramatically at first, if you're good and you've begun from a standing start. But that steep growth and acceleration will eventually flatten out due to limits of the present clients and services, penetration of high-potential prospects, competition, technology, and so on. That plateau will eventually decline because of the laws of entropy.

The time to leap to the next S-curve of dramatic growth is as you are still accelerating (a position of strength), not after you've been on the plateau, where the distance to leap is far greater and you have less momentum (a position of weakness).

REINVENTION CHECKLIST

❑ Timing:

   ❑ Your revenue growth is less than 10 percent over prior year two years running.

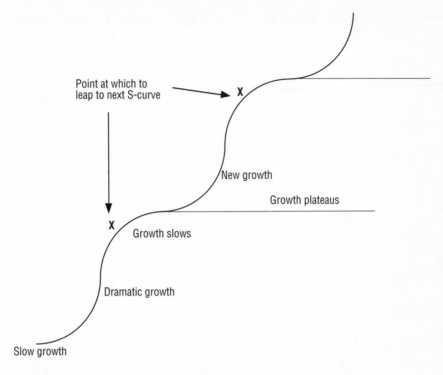

FIGURE 10.1 S-Curve of Consulting Practice Growth

- ❑ Your products and services haven't changed in two years or more.
- ❑ You have not launched a new brand in two years or more.
- ❑ Your new clients over the past two years are less than 20 percent of your business.
- ❑ You are totally comfortable (or even bored) in your delivery and offerings.
- ❑ Potential:
  - ❑ Introduce new products and services to existing clients.
  - ❑ Introduce existing products and services to new clients.

- ❑ Introduce new products and services to new clients (toughest of the three).
- ❑ Create a new brand or several brands.
- ❑ Form new alliances.
- ❑ Write a new book, column, or series of articles.
- ❑ Launch a new web site or radically change the existing one.
- ❑ Reinforcement:
  - ❑ Allot formal and considerable amounts of time to new directions.
  - ❑ Support the new endeavor financially and unstintingly.
  - ❑ Use outside help to launch and fine-tune as necessary.
  - ❑ Create and perpetuate marketing and promotional campaigns.

COMMENTARY

Older, comfortable technology and methodology will tend to subsume newer initiatives. Therefore, there is a need to formally plan, support, and finance the new ventures. Create a new brand and a new look for it, as well.

The stronger your existing brand, visibility, and client base, the stronger your chances of successfully reinventing your practice. That's why it is vital to remember that the best times to change are during times of strength and growth, not out of desperation and need for recovery. Never be conservative or content about your success. Rather, use your success to take prudent risks and test new waters.

The best and most successful consultants never simply sit back and rest on their prior achievements. They are restless.

SELLING YOUR FIRM

There are two basic models for professional services firms:

In the first model the brand is the owner and/or it is a sole practitioner firm (such as mine). As a rule, these firms are simply legal enti-

ties enabling you to withdraw earnings in real time, but do not establish equity over the longer term since the brand is your name and you
are the only asset. The advantage is the ability to withdraw (often very
large) amounts of money on a yearly basis for investment, sustaining a
fine lifestyle, paying for major expenses out of cash flow, and so on.
The disadvantage is that you will not build a salable equity product
over the years.

In the second model the brand is the firm and its proprietary approaches, and there is infrastructure, assets, client goodwill, staff, and
so forth. This means you can leave (sell) the company and under new
leadership its basic operations can continue. The advantage is that you
may build a company that provides millions of dollars for you when
you sell it. The disadvantage is that you will have had to invest signifi-
cantly in the business (as opposed to taking out cash) to build it, hire
and manage staff, and invest in offices and equipment.

Consequently, selling the firm is oriented toward the second business model. Generally, professional services firms sell in the range of
one to two times revenues or four to ten times profits (with the owner's
compensation absorbed into the profit consideration). Occasionally, a
personal brand company as in the first example can be sold, but it is
unusual to do so. Moreover, in either case, there can be a demand that
the owner continue to work for the firm for an extended time under
contract on salary, which is usually the worst of all worlds. If you sell,
make a clean break. The only thing worse than sweating blood for
yourself and your family is doing it for someone else!

SELLING YOUR FIRM CHECKLIST

- ❑ Preparatory work:
    - ❑ Establish time frame well in advance.
    - ❑ Establish contact with veteran intermediary/valuation
      professional.
    - ❑ Orient firm toward maximum valuation potential:
      Reduce expenses.
      Grow top line.

Improve profit line.

Solidify long-term client contracts.

Accelerate new business acquisition.

Renew copyrights, trademarks, registrations, and the like.

Consolidate and update testimonials and references.

❑ Evaluate employee buyout.

❑ Seeking buyers:

  ❑ Consider broker or intermediary.

  ❑ Consider key competition that may want to acquire.

  ❑ Consider key clients who may want to acquire.

  ❑ Let network know: trade associations, former colleagues, insiders.

  ❑ Explore leveraged buyout from employees if interested.

❑ Evaluating buyer (due diligence):

  ❑ Examine buyer finances.

  ❑ Ensure values compatibility (e.g., no mass firings).

  ❑ Ensure your personal disengagement.

  ❑ If leveraged with employees, ensure payment terms and guarantees.

  ❑ Create as simple and cut-and-dried deal as possible.

  ❑ Clarify your future accessibility to consult, any noncompete restrictions, and so on.

  ❑ Clarify what is yours and what is the firm's (included in sale and excluded).

❑ During sale and postsale:

  ❑ Keep employees honestly and accurately informed.

  ❑ Inform clients when sale will be consummated, and create continuity strategy.

  ❑ Inform media and professional contacts/associations.

  ❑ Walk away.

COMMENTARY

If you've built a company to provide equity for you later in life so that you can pursue other interests, then do so. Don't hang around, because it will be terrible for the company, your former employees, and you. Treat a sale as a total departure.

It is tough to sell professional services firms *unless* they exhibit long-term and sustained growth or they possess unique and proprietary approaches to their market (and, of course, both of those conditions would be ideal). The former is more important than the latter in terms of high value, because the former provides instant income for the buyer and the latter requires investment to resuscitate the company if it's not growing (and that investment comes out of your sale price).

The moral: Plan well ahead for your company's sale, focus on the key indexes (in the checklist) that will maximize perceived value, and search for buyers when you can sustain those key values over time. That is the height of your sales potential.

APPENDIX

The United States of America

CERTIFICATE OF REGISTRATION
PRINCIPAL REGISTER

The Mark shown in this certificate has been registered in the United States Patent and Trademark Office to the named registrant.

The records of the United States Patent and Trademark Office show that an application for registration of the Mark shown in this Certificate was filed in the Office; that the application was examined and determined to be in compliance with the requirements of the law and with the regulations prescribed by the Director of the United States Patent and Trademark Office; and that the Applicant is entitled to registration of the Mark under the Trademark Act of 1946, as Amended.

A copy of the Mark and pertinent data from the application are part of this certificate.

This registration shall remain in force for TEN (10) years, unless terminated earlier as provided by law, and subject to compliance with the provisions of Section 8 of the Trademark Act of 1946, as Amended.

Director of the United States Patent and Trademark Office

Example of Trademark Registration

204

SECTION 8: AFFIDAVIT OF CONTINUED USE

The registration shall remain in force for 10 years, except that the
registration shall be canceled for failure to file an Affidavit of Continued
Use under Section 8 of the Trademark Act, 15 U.S.C. §1058, upon the
expiration of the following time periods:
   i) At the end of 6 years following the date of registration.
   ii) At the end of each successive 10-year period following the date of
   registration.

*Failure to file a proper Section 8 Affidavit at the appropriate time will result in the
cancellation of the registration.*

SECTION 9: APPLICATION FOR RENEWAL

The registration shall remain in force for 10 years, subject to the provisions
of Section 8, except that the registration shall expire for failure to file an
Application for Renewal under Section 9 of the Trademark Act, 15 U.S.C.
§1059, at the end of each successive 10-year period following the date of
registration.

*Failure to file a proper Application for Renewal at the appropriate time will result in
the expiration of the registration.*

**No further notice or reminder of these requirements will be sent to the
Registrant by the Patent and Trademark Office. It is recommended
that the Registrant contact the Patent and Trademark Office
approximately one year before the expiration of the time periods shown
above to determine the requirements and fees for the filings required to
maintain the registration.**

Int. Cls.: 16 and 41

Prior U.S. Cls.: 2, 5, 22, 23, 29, 37, 38, 50, 100, 101 and
107

Reg. No. 2,721,113

United States Patent and Trademark Office   Registered June 3, 2003

TRADEMARK
SERVICE MARK
PRINCIPAL REGISTER

BALANCING ACT

SUMMIT CONSULTING GROUP INC. (RHODE
ISLAND CORPORATION)
85 BRISAS CIRCLE
EAST GREENWICH, RI 02818

FOR: NEWSLETTERS CONCERNING MOTIVA-
TION AND SELF-IMPROVEMENT, IN CLASS 16
(U.S. CLS. 2, 5, 22, 23, 29, 37, 38 AND 50).

FIRST USE 9-1-1999; IN COMMERCE 9-1-1999.

FOR: WORKSHOPS IN THE FIELDS OF MOTIVA-
TION, PERSONAL GROWTH, SELF-IMPROVE-
MENT, GOALS AND PRIORITIES AND TIME
MANAGEMENT, IN CLASS 41 (U.S. CLS. 100, 101
AND 107).

FIRST USE 10-1-1999; IN COMMERCE 10-1-1999.

SER. NO. 76-432,162, FILED 7-19-2002.

MICHAEL KEATING, EXAMINING ATTORNEY

Example of Trademark Registration *(Continued)*

"A worldwide expert in executive education."
-- *Success Magazine*

| About Alan Weiss | Services ▾ | On-Line Store ▾ | Free Articles ▾ | Workshops ▾ | Home |

Upcoming Workshops & Seminars

Special Features

THE MILLION DOLLAR
CONSULTING™ COLLEGE
An Intensive Week of
Practice Improvement

October 3-7, 2005, Boston, MA
Click here for more information

See photos and comments
from the first Consulting College.

**Balancing Act Free
Monthly E-Newsletter**

Over 5 years' worth of
life balancing information

Listen to:
"Tools For Change:
The 1% Solution"

You need the Windows Media Player and
Microsoft Internet Explorer to hear this file.

2005 *Teleconference Series*

Alan Weiss
At Festival
Ballet Providence
September 12, 2005

Discuss and Grow

New Audio Package!

Spend a day with Alan Weiss...

The One-Day MBA
Part II

*12 hours of solid career-building advice
you can implement immediately*

Prepublication Discount Offer
Click here to learn more

ALAN'S FORUMS
A destination for entrepreneurs and
professional services providers to improve
their lives, careers, and businesses.

Alan's Forums are open to anyone who registers on an
annual or lifetime basis. It is a site and bulletin board
containing discussions, questions and answers,
articles, and related material for professionals seeking
to improve their careers, business, and lives.

Click here for more information and registration.

Million Dollar Consulting™ Features

| Executive Briefings | Hot Tips | Mentor Program |
| Summit Resource Center | Private Coaching Program | |

Winner: 2004 Axiem Award for Presentation Excellence

The Society for Advancement of Consulting, LLC is an organization founded by
Alan Weiss for the purpose of advancing the success and influence of
independent consultants of all specialties. For information about membership,
click here.

The CMC designation (Certified Management Consultant) is awarded by the
Institute of Management Consultants and represents evidence of the highest
standards of consulting and adherence to the ethical canons of the profession.
Less than 1% of all consultants have achieved this level of performance.

[About Alan Weiss - Services - On-Line Store - Free Articles - Workshops]

E-mail info@summitconsulting.com
P.O. Box 1009
East Greenwich, RI 02818-0964
Telephone: (401) 884-2778
Fax: (401) 884-5068

All pages developed by: WebEditor Design Services

Alan's Daughter's Wedding

Example of Web Site Home Page

BIBLIOGRAPHY

GENERAL BUSINESS AND CONSULTING

Argyris, Chris. *Integrating the Individual and the Organization*. New York: John Wiley & Sons, 1964.
> Work by a prolific writer and preeminent psychologist on combining positive team-building with individual well-being to create improved performance.

Bellman, Geoffrey. *The Consultant's Calling*. San Francisco: Jossey-Bass, 1990.
> One of the philosophic books on consulting you should read. Geoff focuses on the philosophy and values of the profession.

Bennis, Warren, and Burt Nanus. *The Unconscious Conspiracy: Why Leaders Can't Lead*. New York: Amacom, 1976.
> The original and still best work by Bennis on leadership. Everything else he's done is really a variation of this work and its "leaders are made" philosophy.

Drucker, Peter. *The Effective Executive*. New York: Harper & Row, 1966.
> This is still a powerful work, and probably Drucker's best.

Drucker, Peter. *Managing in the New Society*. New York: St. Martin's Press, 2002.
> This series of essays, each on a highly provocative topic, demonstrates that Drucker is still on top of his game in his 90s.

Fiedler, Frederick. *A Theory of Leadership Effectiveness*. New York: McGraw-Hill, 1967.
> The champion, perhaps, of the contingency theory approach to leadership.

Gabor, Andrea. *The Capitalist Philosophers*. New York: Crown Publishing Group, 2000.
> An extraordinary set of brief biographies, from Mary Parker Follett to Elton Mayo and Peter Drucker. This has been required reading in my graduate classes.

Gardner, John. *On Leadership*. New York: Free Press, 1990.
> Simply one of the best, most succinct writers on the subject.

Gibson, James, et al. *Organizations*. New York: Irwin, 2000.

> An excellent graduate-level text.

Gilbert, Tom. *Human Competence*. New York: McGraw-Hill, 1978.

> Work carried on by Geary Rummler today. Focus on the performer as part of a stimulus-response dynamic.

Jay, Antony. *Management and Machiavelli*. New York: Bantam, 1967.

> Enjoyable and lucid discussion of politics and maneuvering in organizational cultures.

Likert, Rensis. *New Patterns of Management*. New York: McGraw-Hill, 1970.

> One of the toughest writers to comprehend; nevertheless his studies on leadership and performance led to some groundbreaking work at the University of Michigan.

Mager, Robert. *The Mager Library*. Belmont, CA: Pittman Learning, 1984.

> If you haven't read the collected—and insightfully funny—works of Mager, you aren't educated in this industry.

Maslow, Abraham. *Motivation and Personality*. New York: Harper & Row, 1970.

> Classic work on hierarchy of needs and human motivation.

McClelland, David. *Human Motivation*. Cambridge: Cambridge University Press, 1985.

> Need/achievement theory and connections to Maslow's work.

McGregor, David. *The Human Side of Enterprise*. New York: McGraw-Hill, 1960.

> McGregor's classic work on Theory X and Theory Y.

Sampson, Anthony. *The Company Man*. New York: Times Business, 1995.

> A good history of companies, organizations, and the reasons for their current structure.

Schein, Edgar. *Process Consultation*. Reading, MA: Addison-Wesley, 1969.

> Still *the* authority on process consultation.

Taylor, Frederick Winslow. *Scientific Management*. New York: Harper, 1911.

> This is a terrific book, by the first management consultant. A must read if you're serious about the profession.

Vroom, Victor, and Philip Yetton. *Leadership and Decision Making.* Pittsburgh, PA: University of Pittsburgh Press, 1973.

> More recent work is available, but this is their seminal book on situational leadership. It's tough sledding. Often referred to as "normative" or "path/goal" theory.

Weiss, Alan. *Getting Started in Consulting.* 2nd ed. Hoboken, NJ: John Wiley & Sons, 2004.

> A narrative, sequential journey to start a practice from square zero, covering everything from the cost of office equipment to gaining repeat business.

Weiss, Alan. *Million Dollar Consulting: The Professional's Guide to Building a Practice.* 3rd ed. New York: McGraw-Hill, 2002.

> Still my best seller after all these years.

Zaleznik, Abraham. *The Managerial Mystique.* New York: Harper & Row, 1989.

> One of the most vocal in terms of "leaders are born, not made." A counterpoint to the work of Bennis.

COLD CALLS

Boyan, Lee. *Successful Cold Call Selling.* 2nd ed. New York: Amacom, 1989.

> Scripts for nearly every contingency, tips for dealing with receptionists and gatekeepers, useful questions to ask, and so on.

Geraghty, Barbara. *Visionary Selling: How to Get to Top Executives—and How to Sell Them When You're There.* New York: Simon & Schuster, 1998.

> How to meet and mingle with top executives, what to say, how to say it, and how to bridge from meeting to closing.

Goldner, Paul S. *Red-Hot Cold Call Selling: Prospecting Techniques That Pay Off.* New York: Amacom, 1995.

> Prospecting and making contact over the phone. How to gain attention quickly and how to prevent phone calls from killing you.

Heiman, Stephen E., et al. *The New Strategic Selling*. New York: Warner, 1998.

 A semiclassic, one of the original references to an "economic buyer." Focuses on both strategy and tactics for escaping the gatekeeper.

Rackham, Neil. *SPIN Selling*. New York: McGraw-Hill, 1988.

 This has become a cult classic in terms of scientific studies of what prompts people to accept calls and to make buying decisions. "SPIN" stands awkwardly for "situation, problem, implication, and need-payoff."

Weiss, Alan. *How to Acquire Clients*. San Francisco: Jossey-Bass/Pfeiffer, 2002.

 My fourth book in the Ultimate Consultant series focuses on a systematic selling sequence, the next "yes," and adapting to various buyers' styles.

PUBLISHING ASSISTANCE

Brogan, Kathryn S., *2005 Writer's Market: 4,000 Places to Sell What You Write!* Cincinnati, OH: Writer's Digest Books, 2005.

 A treasury of more than 4,000 listings for magazines, books, journals, and so on, plus interviews, self-marketing tips.

Herman, Deborah Levine, and Jeff Herman. *Write the Perfect Book Proposal: 10 That Sold and Why*. New York: John Wiley & Sons, 2001.

 How to organize, sell, and dramatize your ideas for maximum effect.

Herman, Jeff. *Jeff Herman's Guide to Book Publishers, Editors, and Literary Agents, 2005: Who They Are! What They Want! And How to Win Them Over!* New York: Jeff Herman, 2005.

 Ultimate reference on who's who in the writing industry and how to reach them.

Larsen, Michael. *How to Write a Book Proposal*. 3rd ed. Cincinnati, OH: Writers Digest Books, 1997.

 Step-by-step help in creating chapters, getting editors' attention, and overall structure.

101 QUESTIONS FOR ANY SALES SITUATION YOU'LL EVER FACE

AN OVERVIEW

This material is intended to provide questions to ask in virtually any sales situation, thereby:

✔ Maintaining a conversational and nonsales approach.

✔ Keeping the other party talking in order to learn.

✔ Avoiding "deselection" by volunteering very little yourself.

✔ Finding the buyer, building a relationship, and closing business.

✔ Accelerating the entire sales process.

The questions are deliberately overlapping, and stop just short of duplicative. Essentially, you want to elicit the same information in as many diverse ways as possible.

A FEW GUIDELINES FOR USE

✔ Don't interrogate people. It's seldom necessary to ask even the majority of questions in any one category.

✔ Employ follow-up questions. The questions contained herein are triggers that may engender a response that demands further clarification.

✔ Trust is essential for candor. The other party will be most honest and responsive when trust is established (e.g., they believe you have their best interests in mind).

✔ Never be content with a single question, no matter how satisfying the answer appears to be. Some people will attempt to deceive you to save their ego, and others will inadvertently deceive you because they misunderstood the question. I recommend that you use at least three questions per category if the answers are consistent, and six or more if the answers appear to be inconsistent.

Qualifying the Prospect

This is the process of determining whether the prospect is appropriate for your business in terms of size, relevance, seriousness, and related factors. In other words, you don't want to pursue a lead that can't result in legitimate—and worthwhile—business.

Questions

1. Why do you think we might be a good match?
2. Is there a budget allocated for this project?
3. How important is this need (on a scale of 1 to 10)?
4. What is your timing to accomplish this?
5. Who, if anyone, is demanding that this be accomplished?
6. How soon are you willing to begin?
7. Have you made a commitment to proceed, or are you still analyzing?
8. What are your key decision criteria in choosing a resource?
9. Have you tried this before (will this be a continuing endeavor)?
10. Is your organization seeking formal proposals for this work?

Key Point: You want to determine whether the potential work is large enough for your involvement, relevant to your expertise, and near enough on the horizon to merit rapid responsiveness.

Finding the Economic Buyer

The economic buyer is the person who can write a check in return for your value contribution. He or she is the *only* buyer to be concerned about. Contrary to a great deal of poor advice, the economic buyer is virtually *never* in human resources, training, meeting planning, or related support areas.

QUESTIONS

11. Whose budget will support this initiative?

12. Who can immediately approve this project?

13. To whom will people look for support, approval, and credibility?

14. Who controls the resources required to make this happen?

15. Who has initiated this request?

16. Who will claim responsibility for the results?

17. Who will be seen as the main sponsor and/or champion?

18. Do you have to seek anyone else's approval?

19. Who will accept or reject proposals?

20. If you and I were to shake hands, could I begin tomorrow?

Key Point: The larger the organization, the more economic buyers there will be. They need not be the CEO or owner, but must be able to authorize and produce payment. Committees are *never* economic buyers.

REBUTTING OBJECTIONS

"Obstacles are those terrible things you see when you take your eyes off the goal," said philosopher Hannah Arendt. Objections are a sign of *interest*. Turn them around to your benefit. Once you demolish objections, there is no longer a reason not to proceed in a partnership.

QUESTIONS (IN RESPONDING TO AN ECONOMIC BUYER'S OBJECTIONS)

21. Why do you feel that way? (Get at the true cause.)

22. If we resolve this, can we then proceed? (Is this the sole objection?)

23. But isn't that exactly why you need me? (The reversal approach.)

24. What would satisfy you? (Make the buyer answer the objection.)

25. What can we do to overcome that? (Demonstrate joint accountability.)

26. Is this unique? (Is there a precedent for overcoming it?)

27. What's the consequence? (Is it really serious or merely an annoyance?)

28. Isn't that low-probability? (Worry about likelihoods, not remote possibilities.)

29. Shall I address that in the proposal? (Let's focus on value.)

30. Why does it even matter in light of the results? (The return on investment is the point.)

Key Point: Don't be on the defensive by trying to slay each objection with your sword, or you'll eventually fall on it. Embrace the buyer in the solutions, and demonstrate that some objections are insignificant when compared with benefits (e.g., there will always be some unhappy employees in any change effort).

ESTABLISHING OBJECTIVES

Objectives are the *outcomes* that represent the client's desired and improved conditions. They are never inputs (e.g., reports, focus groups, manuals) but rather always outputs (e.g., increased sales, reduced attrition, improved teamwork). Clear objectives prevent scope creep and enable a rational engagement and disengagement to take place, resulting in much greater consulting efficiency and profit margins. (Note that the questions dealing with objectives, and value are the basis of conceptual agreement.)

QUESTIONS

31. What is the ideal outcome you'd like to experience?

32. What results are you trying to accomplish?

33. What better product/service/customer condition are you seeking?

34. Why are you seeking to do this (work/project/engagement)?

35. How would the operation be different as a result of this work?

36. What would be the return on investment (sales, assets, equity, etc.)?

37. How would image/reputation/credibility be improved?

38. What harm (e.g., stress, dysfunction, turf wars, etc.) would be alleviated?

39. How much would you gain on the competition as a result?

40. How would your value proposition be improved?

Key Point: Most buyers know what they *want* but not necessarily what they *need*. By pushing the buyer on the end results, you are helping to articulate and formalize the client's perceived benefits, thereby increasing your own value in the process. Without clear objectives you do not have a legitimate project.

ESTABLISHING METRICS

Metrics are measures of progress toward the objectives that enable you and the client to ascertain the rate and totality of success. They assign proper credit to you and your efforts, and also signify when the project is complete (objectives are met) and it is proper to disengage.

QUESTIONS

41. How will you know we've accomplished your intent?

42. How, specifically, will the operation be different when we're done?

43. How will you measure this?

44. What indicators will you use to assess our progress?

45. Who or what will report on our results (against the objectives)?

46. Do you already have measures in place you intend to apply?

47. What is the rate of return (on sales, investment, etc.) that you seek?

48. How will we know the public, employees, and/or customers perceive the change?

49. Each time we talk, what standard will tell us we're progressing?

50. How would you know it if you tripped over it?

Key Point: Measures can be subjective, so long as you and the client agree on who is doing the measuring and how. For example, the buyer's observation that he or she is called upon less to settle turf disputes and has fewer complaints from direct reports aimed at colleagues are valid measures for the objective of improved teamwork.

ASSESSING VALUE

Determining the value of the project for the client's organization is the most critical aspect of conceptual agreement and preproposal interaction. That's because when the buyer stipulates a significant value, the fee is placed in proper perspective (return on investment) and is seldom an issue of contention. Conversations with the buyer should always focus on value and never on fee or price.

QUESTIONS

51. What will these results mean for your organization?

52. How would you assess the actual return (return on investment, return on assets, return on sales, return on equity, etc.)?

53. What would be the extent of the improvement (or correction)?

54. How will these results impact the bottom line?

55. What are the annualized savings (first year might be deceptive)?

56. What is the intangible impact (e.g., on reputation, safety, comfort, etc.)?

57. How would you, personally, be better off or better supported?

58. What is the scope of the impact (on customers, employees, vendors)?

59. How important is this compared to your overall responsibilities?

60. What if this fails?

Key Points: Subjective value (stress alleviated) can be every bit as important as more tangible results (higher sales). Never settle for "Don't worry, it's important." Find out *how* important, because that will dictate the acceptable fee range.

DETERMINING THE BUDGET RANGE

Too much guessing takes place in the absence of a general understanding about how much the prospect intends to invest (prior to understanding the full value proposition). In many cases, the budget is fixed and entirely inappropriate, and in others it represents a better understanding of the return on investment than that of the consultant! (Don't forget, this presupposes you're talking to an economic buyer.)

QUESTIONS

61. Have you arrived at a budget or investment range for this project?

62. Are funds allocated, or must they be requested?

63. What is your expectation of the investment required?

64. So we don't waste time, are there parameters to remain within?

65. Have you done this before, and at what investment level?

66. What are you able to authorize during this fiscal year?

67. Can I assume that a strong proposition will justify proper expenditure?

68. How much are you prepared to invest to gain these dramatic results?

69. For a dramatic return, will you consider a larger investment?

70. Let's be frank: What are you willing to spend?

Key Points: There is nothing wrong with exceeding the budget expectation if you muster a strong enough value proposition. But don't even proceed with a proposal if the prospect has a seriously misguided expectation of the investment need, or simply has an inadequate fixed budget.

PREVENTING UNFORESEEN OBSTACLES

As comedienne Gilda Radner used to say, "It's always something." Inevitably, it seems, the best-laid plans are undermined by objections, occurrences, and happenings from left field. Fortunately, there are questions to establish some preventive actions against even the unforeseen.

QUESTIONS

71. Is there anything we haven't discussed that could get in the way?

72. In the past, what has occurred to derail potential projects like this?

73. What haven't I asked you that I should have about the environment?

74. What do you estimate the probability is of our going forward?

75. Are you surprised by anything I've said or that we've agreed upon?

76. At this point, are you still going to make this decision yourself?

77. What, if anything, do you additionally need to hear from me?

78. Is anything likely to change in the organization in the near future?

79. Are you awaiting the results of any other initiatives or decisions?

80. If I get this proposal to you tomorrow, how soon will you decide?

Key Points: Make sure that your project isn't contingent upon other events transpiring (or not transpiring). If the buyer is holding out on you, these questions will make it more difficult to dissemble. Build into your proposal benefits to outweigh the effects of any external factors.

INCREASING THE SIZE OF THE SALE

Once conceptual agreement is gained, it makes sense to capitalize on the common ground and strive for the largest possible relationship. Most consultants don't obtain larger contracts because they don't ask for or suggest them. You can't possibly lose anything attempting to increase the business at this juncture.

QUESTIONS

81. Would you be amenable to my providing a variety of options?

82. Is this the only place (division, department, geography) applicable?

83. Would it be wise to extend this through implementation and oversight?

84. Should we plan to also coach key individuals essential to the project?

85. Would you benefit from benchmarking against other firms?

86. Would you also like an idea of what a retainer might look like?

87. Are there others in your position with like needs I should see?

88. Do your subordinates possess the skills to support you appropriately?

89. Should we run focus groups/other sampling to test employee reactions?

90. Would you like me to test customer response at various stages?

Key Points: If you don't ask, you don't get. Don't throw everything including the kitchen sink into your proposal in an attempt to justify your fee. Instead, "unbundle" what you're capable of providing and add it back in at an additional fee.

GOING FOR THE CLOSE

You're in the home stretch, but not across the finish line. Runners who slow up at the approaching tape lose to someone else with a better late kick. Run through the tape at full speed by driving the conversation right through the close of the sale and the check clearing the bank.

QUESTIONS

91. If the proposal reflects our last discussions, how soon can we begin?

92. Is it better to start immediately, or wait for the first of the month?

93. Is there anything at all preventing our working together at this point?

94. How rapidly are you prepared to begin once you see the proposal?

95. If you get the proposal tomorrow, can I call Friday morning at 10 for approval?

96. While I'm here, should I begin some of the preliminary work today?

97. Would you like to shake hands and get started, proposal to follow?

98. Do you prefer to issue a corporate check or to wire the funds electronically?

99. May I allocate two days early next week to start my interviews?

100. Can we proceed?

Key Points: There is never a better time than when you're in front of the buyer and he or she is in agreement and excited about the project. Even without a proposal, beginning immediately cements the conceptual agreement and greatly diminishes the possibility of being derailed by surprise.

THE MOST VITAL QUESTION

All of the preceding 100 questions are actually based on the reaction to one question that we often fail to ask of the most difficult person of all. And unlike most of the prior inquiries, it's a simple binary question, with a clear "yes" or "no" response.

QUESTION

101. Do you believe it yourself?

Key Point: The first sale is always to yourself.

SAMPLE POSITION PAPER OR WHITE PAPER

ACCEPTING EQUITY FOR YOUR SERVICES: OR WHY THE CRAPS TABLES SUDDENLY LOOK GOOD

Alan Weiss, PhD

Consultants (and a raft of other professionals, including carpenters and plumbers) are increasingly considering equity participation in place of old-fashioned cash on the barrelhead. Sometimes it's because the clients can't (or claim they can't) come up with the cash, and sometimes it's because the allure of the client's potential payoff is so great that vast riches clog the consultant's synapses.

Equity offers exist in two basic situations: In the first, the company is a start-up, usually high-tech but not always, which is so cash poor that it can only apply the precious venture capital for R&D and marketing. Anything else is superfluous, so everyone from accountants to gardeners is offered a stake. In the second case, a legitimate going concern offers a consultant the chance to participate in the fruits of his or her advice, usually because the client thinks the chances of reaching the goal are slim, doesn't want to pay for anything but tangible performance, or is simply cheap.

In either case, there is a strong and rare potential upside, and a strong and frequent absolute downside. Let the equity seeker beware (caveat equitus, or something).

What You Need to Know

Before you jump to accept an equity position, you should make sure that you possess the basic information about the client *and* about yourself. In any given instance, equity can make sense for you and not a partner, or vice versa. In other words, this is like driving a Ferrari: It seems like a great idea and you know you'll look good, but not everyone can handle it and there are some places you just can't take it.

Is It Light or an Approaching Train?

You have more of a chance of hitting a roulette number during an evening at the tables than you do hitting the big time with an equity start-up. Even in established organizations, where you're taking equity on increased sales or growing market share, there are hazards.

You'll have to get a reading on the likelihood of key talent staying the course. That means that you'll also have to be absolutely confident about management's ability to lead and to retain key people. Look at the culture. Is it one of relatively low turnover (no turnover is not good, since it fails to clear deadwood), fun, challenge, and collaboration? Are people talking about the excitement of the enterprise, not about the potential for jumping ship?

Is the initiative capitalized sufficiently? Are resources and knowledge readily available and shared? Are people running at full speed to gain momentum (or to flee a fire)? Ask yourself whether the operation in which you are considering taking an equity position is one that you would enjoy working in and/or managing. Ask yourself whether you would invest $50,000 of discretionary funds in this opportunity, because that's precisely what you're doing.

Do you like these people and do you trust them?

Who's in Charge?

Your deal about equity must be clear-cut and as unambiguous as possible. The chief executive officer (CEO) and the chief financial officer (CFO) of the client should sign off on the agreement, which itself should be created by your attorney. If the client insists on his or her own attorneys, then agree only with the provision that your attorney will then review their work. Sometimes seemingly trivial matters, such as the state in which legal disputes will be adjudicated, can make a huge difference later (some jurisdictions have laws that could make your position untenable and your contract worthless under certain conditions).

Use as much "cement" as possible to seal the deal. For example, if there is a board of directors, have the agreement approved by the board and read into the minutes. If key personnel change—especially likely in start-up companies—then have the new officer acknowledge and sign off on the old agreement, even though technically it is binding even without that signature.

What's Your Stress Level?

Evaluate the opportunity not in terms of an individual investment but in terms of your overall cash flow and financial picture. Can you support yourself and your business adequately without the equity position paying off? If not, then you're creating a huge gamble. If so, then you're taking a prudent risk. Determine whether you can simply let this run its course, albeit with you contributing as a consultant, or if you'd be up during the night and distracted during the day trying to worry this venture over the finish line.

There is no sense getting sick over a piece of business. You have to be careful that, even if the equity position pays off, it doesn't totally undermine all of your other marketing and delivery efforts, which may suffer by comparison.

What You Need to Do

There are some very specific things you can do to protect yourself in equity relationships. They don't always work, just like fire protection doesn't always work, but at least it's better than simply depending on the sprinkler system.

Evaluate Your Conflicts of Interest

The absolutely toughest factor in taking equity is that it can color your judgment and blunt your effectiveness as a consultant, ironically causing you to become detrimental to your own interests. For example, you might come upon a manager who you know is toxic and ought to be fired. But will you recommend firing him or her, even though it's essential for long-term success, if the position won't be filled for months and you desperately need a body in it to make this year's plan? How much of the future do you sacrifice to guarantee your short-term equity stake?

The answer, if course, is that you have to do what's in the best long-term interests of the client, and not the best short-term financial interest of the consultant. Understand this and evaluate the potential for conflict at the outset. If you anticipate such a conflict, either don't take the job or refer all such decisions to consultants or insiders who don't have the conflict, and abide by their decisions.

Establish What You Can and Can't Control

You may do everything humanly possible within your accountabilities, and the contribution should have led to success. But the unanticipated resignation of three top salespeople, the competition's breathtaking new technology, or the government's unexpected regulatory interference might send a torpedo into your best efforts. Try to clarify what you can and can't control. You won't be able to collect if the goals aren't met no matter what your contribution (because there will be no equity to share), so if you find this potential high, don't get in the water.

You may also find that there are managers or highly influential contributors who are rewarded, directly or indirectly, for the exact opposite of what you are trying to accomplish (e.g., a marketing vice president wants to incorporate sales into his unit, and would love to see the expansion in Europe fail so that he can make a case for the integration). If those turf battles are present, you're going to get killed in the crossfire.

Set an Example of Proper Conduct

Throughout the project, act as you always should—as an independent, objective, and decisive adviser. Don't allow yourself to be persuaded by short-term scares, and never enter into discussions that might indicate your judgment is suspect (or can be bought). Make some tough calls early, if possible, to show that your only objective is to improve the client's condition for the long term.

If you're working with a start-up, confront management often and early. These entrepreneurs have a chronically narrow view. They can see their technology and its implications, and can rarely see the market, the buyer, or the elusive profit goals (known as spending less than you take in). If you're working with a large organization in a specific initiative (for example, the sales force and its business growth), then make sure you become very familiar with every key player. Never simply accept someone's word about someone else's performance or morale. See it for yourself.

Review Each Situation, Well, Situationally

If someone at IBM wants to offer you IBM stock in return for your consulting efforts, that's far different from someone at Silverware.com wanting you to take equity in their new electric fork. Equity in a blue-chip company is like investing in the best market stocks and funds: If you hold on without panic, the market ultimately rewards you. But do you want to either invest in a high-tech start-up or take your chances with factors you can never completely control with a more mature organization? It depends on your tolerance for risk, your eye for opportunity, and your consulting expertise. And on luck.

Don't be afraid to take equity, but don't do it in lieu of cash you need to support your loved ones and your business.

About the Author

Alan Weiss, PhD, is the author of 24 books, including *Million Dollar Consulting*. He has consulted with organizations such as Mercedes-Benz, Fleet Bank, Merck, and Hewlett-Packard, and delivers about 50 keynotes speeches a year. Visit his web site, www.summitconsulting.com, and e-mail him at info@summitconsulting.com.

INDEX

—— About the Author ——

Alan Weiss is one of those rare people who can say he is a consultant, speaker, and author and mean it. His consulting firm, Summit Consulting Group, Inc., has attracted clients such as Merck, Hewlett-Packard, General Electric, Mercedes-Benz, State Street Corporation, Times Mirror Group, the Federal Reserve, the *New York Times*, and more than 500 other leading organizations. He serves on the national board of directors of the Institute of Management Consultants, as well as the boards of Trinity Repertory Company (a Tony Award–winning New England regional theater), the Newport (RI) International Film Festival, and the Harvard Center for Mental Health and the Media. He is the founder and CEO of the Society for Advancement of Consulting, dedicated to improving the business and influence of professional services providers.

His speaking typically includes 50 keynotes a year at major conferences, and he has been a visiting faculty member at Case Western Reserve University, Boston College, Tufts, St. John's University, the University of Illinois, the Institute of Management Studies, and the University of Georgia Graduate School of Business. He has held an appointment as adjunct professor in the Graduate School of Business at the University of Rhode Island, where he taught courses on advanced management and consulting skills. He holds the record for selling out the highest-priced workshop (on entrepreneurialism) in the 22-year history of New York City's Learning Annex. His PhD is in psychology and he is a member of the American Psychological Society, the American Counseling Association, the Society for Personality and Social Psychology, and Division 13 of the American Psychological Association.

His prolific publishing includes more than 500 articles and 24 books, including his best seller, *Million Dollar Consulting* (from McGraw-Hill). His newest books are *Organizational Development* (John

Wiley & Sons) and *Life Balance: How to Convert Professional Success into Personal Happiness* (Jossey-Bass/Pfeiffer). His books have been on the curricula at Villanova, Temple University, and the Wharton School of Business, and have been translated into German, Italian, Arabic, Spanish, Russian, and Chinese.

He is interviewed and quoted frequently in the media, and is an active member of the American Federation of Television and Radio Artists. His career has taken him to 54 countries and 49 states. (He is afraid to go to North Dakota.) *Success* magazine has cited him in an editorial devoted to his work as "a worldwide expert in executive education." The *New York Post* calls him "one of the most highly regarded independent consultants in America." The National Bureau of Certified Consultants cited him in 2003 as "the foremost consultant and author in the country who is consulting to management." In international competition, he was the recipient of the 2004 Axiem Award for Excellence in Audio Presentation.

He once appeared on the popular TV game show *Jeopardy*, where he lost badly in the first round to a dancing waiter from Iowa.

Visit his web site, www.summitconsulting.com, and e-mail him at info @summitconsulting.com.